Critical Memory

Georgia Southern University

Jack N. and Addie D. Averitt

Lecture Series Number 8

Critical Memory

Public Spheres,

African American Writing,

and Black Fathers and

Sons in America

Houston A. Baker Jr.

The University of Georgia Press   *Athens and London*

© 2001 by the University of Georgia Press
Athens, Georgia 30602
All rights reserved
Designed by Kathi Dailey Morgan
Set in 10 on 15 Minion
Printed and bound by Thomson-Shore, Inc.
The paper in this book meets the guidelines for
permanence and durability of the Committee on
Production Guidelines for Book Longevity of the
Council on Library Resources.

Printed in the United States of America

05   04   03   02   01   C   5   4   3   2   1

Library of Congress Cataloging-in-Publication Data
Baker, Houston A.
Critical memory : public spheres, African American writing,
and Black fathers and sons in America / Houston A. Baker, Jr.
p. cm. — (Jack N. and Addie D. Averitt lecture series ; no. 8)
Includes bibliographical references.
ISBN 0-8203-2240-7 (alk. paper)
1. Afro-Americans—Social conditions. 2. Afro-American men
—Social conditions. 3. Fathers and sons—United States.
4. Afro-Americans—Intellectual life. 5. United States—Race
relations. 6. Memory—Social aspect—United States.
7. American literature—Afro-American authors.
8. Afro-American men in literature. 9. Fathers and sons
in literature. 10. Racism in literature. I. Title. II. Series.
E185.86.B256 2001
305.896′073—dc21   00-045142

British Library Cataloging-in-Publication Data available

Once again . . . for Mark

that he may live in the light

Comparing them by their faculties of memory, reason and imagination, it appears to me, that in memory they are equal to whites. . . .

—Thomas Jefferson, *Notes on the State of Virginia*

If history were the past, history wouldn't matter. History is the present, the present.

You and I are history.

—James Baldwin, *A Rap on Race*

Contents

Foreword

In October 1997, Dr. Houston A. Baker Jr., one of America's preeminent critics of African American literature, delivered the Averitt Lectures on the campus of Georgia Southern University. The Averitt Lectures were established in 1990 by Jack N. and Addie D. Averitt with the purpose of bringing world-class scholars to Georgia Southern to speak on subjects in the fields of history and literature. To date, James Olney, Tony Tanner, Barbara Hardy, and Houston A. Baker Jr. have lectured on literature, presenting to the university their insights on many different writers including Emily Dickinson, Walt Whitman, Gerard Manley Hopkins, Henry James, Dylan Thomas, W. E. B. Du Bois, Booker T. Washington, Richard Wright, and Ralph Ellison. Houston A. Baker Jr.'s talks, by turns challenging, amusing, and provocative, were a superb addition to the Averitt Lectures. Revised and expanded, they form the basis for this present volume.

Houston A. Baker Jr. currently holds a professorship at Duke University. Before that, he was Director of the Center for the Study of Black Literature and Culture, Professor of English, and Albert M. Greenfield Professor at the University of Pennsylvania. A prolific critic, scholar, and writer, Dr. Baker has written numerous reviews, articles, and books, among which are *Workings of the Spirit: The Poetics of Afro-American Women's Writing* (University of Chicago Press, 1991) and *Black Studies, Rap, and the Academy* (University of Chicago Press, 1993). He has received many honors and fellowships, including a Guggenheim Fellowship and a Rockefeller Foundation Fellowship. In 1992, he was elected president of the Modern Language Association, making him the first black person to hold that office in the organization's more than 100-year history. A popular lecturer, Dr. Baker has spoken at the University of Michigan, Cornell University, Purdue University, and at Tuskegee University, where he delivered the First Annual Ralph Ellison Lecture in 1995. Georgia Southern University counts itself honored to have hosted Houston Baker as the 1997 Averitt Lecturer.

As Chair of the 1997 Averitt Lecture Committee, I owe thanks to many people who worked hard on the myriad tasks both large and small that form the unobtrusive yet essential platform upon which any visiting lecturer to a large university ultimately stands. Accordingly, I express my gratitude to my committee members Phyllis Dallas, Richard Flynn, Patsy Griffin, Mildred Pate, Candy Schille, and Terry Thompson. I must give especial praise to Phyllis and Mildred for cheerfully undertaking the lioness's share of the detailed effort involved in the writing, printing, collating, and distribution of invitations and programs. Thanks also to Virginia Spell for providing the spectacularly beautiful flowers and to Helen Cannon, innkeeper and hostess par excellence. Finally, I thank Jack and Addie Averitt for their longstanding devotion to Georgia Southern University and for their generosity in providing the university with a lecture series as fine as the one which appropriately bears their names.

David L. Dudley
Associate Professor of Literature and Philosophy

Preface

The meditation that follows grew out of the Jack N. and Addie D. Averitt Lectures I presented at Georgia Southern University in the fall of 1997. I appreciate the courtesies shown by colleagues and students in Georgia. Their responses and insights shaped my subsequent preparation of the lectures for publication. I believe the urgency of the present social situation in the United States—especially with respect to black fathers and sons—that marked my performances in Georgia has not abated as we enter the new millennium. I realize social urgency often produces polemic. Certainly, a polemical cast marks the following pages. However, it has seemed in my more than thirty years in academia that raising a hue and cry about perceived social injustices seldom causes harm.

The lecture format of my presentations in Georgia, and my avoidance of protocols of a full-length scholarly study, condition both the memoiristic and informal turns of the following pages. I hope to pursue themes and arguments of the present work in more exhaustive and formal accounts—accounts, in fact, that are already in progress.

Meanwhile, I wish to thank all who made the present work possible, especially all at Georgia Southern University and the University of Georgia Press. As well, I want to thank my good friend and colleague Eric Cheyfitz for "staying with me" through various turns and reconfigurations of the Americas Cultural Studies work in which we are mutually engaged. I wish to thank the former chair of my former department, namely Professor Wendy Steiner of the University of Pennsylvania. Her administrative largesse helped make this project possible. I would be deeply remiss if I failed to acknowledge the very important assistance of Mr. Bo Ketner in the preparation of the manuscript. Finally, I owe my deepest debt to my wife Charlotte Pierce-Baker, who always understands.

Acknowledgments

Portions of the following manuscript appeared in *Black Renaissance/Renaissance Noire*, published by Indiana University Press, and in the *Stanford Humanities Review: Movements of the Avant-Garde* 7.1. I wish to thank both journals for permission to reprint. The research assistance of Adam Hotek and James Peterson was indispensable. And the support and caring of my former administrative assistant, Ms. Henrietta Stephens, were invaluable.

Excerpts from "Ole Lem" from *The Collected Poems of Sterling A. Brown*, edited by Michael S. Harper, ©1980 by Sterling A. Brown, are published by permission of HarperCollins Publishers.

Black Modernity

Kitchen Memories,

Likable Black Boys, and

the American South

Alabama made me so upset,

Tennessee would not let me rest,

But everybody knows about Mississippi,

Goddam!

—Nina Simone, "Mississippi Goddam"

In his autobiography, *Black Boy*, Richard Wright describes his experience on one of the first service jobs he occupied as a raw immigrant from the American South:

> After an idle week, I got a job as a dishwasher in a North Side cafe that had just opened. My boss, a white woman, directed me in unpacking barrels of dishes, setting up new tables, painting, and so on. . . . The cook was an elderly Finnish woman with a sharp, bony face. There were several white waitresses. I was the only Negro in the cafe.[1]

One morning, Richard hears the white cook cough and spit: "My senses told me that Tillie had coughed and spat into that pot, but my heart told me that no human being could possibly be so filthy" (274). *Denial* is Wright's instinctive response.

But denial will not do. Wright watches more closely and sickeningly observes that the white cook is actually spitting in the food, creating a horrible situation. And yet, there is a dilemma for the black observer:

> Should I tell the boss lady? Would she believe me? I watched Tillie for another day to make sure that she was spitting in the food. She was; there was no doubt of it. But who would believe me if I told them what was happening? I was the only black person in the cafe.

Perhaps they would think I hated the cook? I stopped eating my
meals there and bided my time. (274)

A lone black boy with a disturbing story to tell about filthy prac-
tices threatening the well-being of all at the table must wait in
silence.

Ironically, it is only when a "Negro girl" is hired to work in the
bustling and ever-more-successful cafe that the story of Tillie may
possibly be told. ("Negro girl," like "black boy," offers some clue
about why black men and women in the United States like their
own Ebonics better than a standard English menu of names.)
Wright confides his observations about the white cook to the
young black woman, and she in turn tells the white boss. What is
the white boss's response? "She said I was crazy.... She just looked
at me with those gray eyes of hers [and said] 'Why would Tillie
do that?'" (276). Again, denial rules the day. But after checking
the young black woman's story with Richard, the owner secretly
watches the cook, discovering the dreadful truth.

But what a time this all takes! How complex and torturous the
process of revelation and possible remedy! It would appear to be
very complex when the crime, corruption, or filth is discovered
by a black man. It seems difficult, as Wright relates the tale, for
him and his black coworker to break through the white boss's
American innocence—even to contribute to the general health
and welfare. Having been told by a white Mississippi employer
early in his southern work life, "Get out, nigger! I don't like your
looks" (182), Richard is understandably reluctant to take responsibility for job-site revelations in the North. He is a black, unskilled
immigrant worker. His prospects for alternative employment
during the American 1930s are not great. And the fact that he has
been able to take his meals at work has been an inestimable benefit
to his family, a family barely able to purchase food for its own daily

subsistence. The revelation of white wrongdoing, like securing food for survival, has always been a difficult business at best for the black majority in the United States.

I take Wright's anecdotal story of the white cook and the American cafe as a vivid and compelling shorthand for what could be presented in abstract philosophical terms about the relationship between black talk and American society. Wright observes elsewhere in *Black Boy*:

> Culturally the Negro represents a paradox: Though he is an organic part of the nation, he is excluded by the entire tide and direction of American culture. Frankly, it is felt to be right to exclude him, and it is felt to be wrong to admit him freely. Therefore if, within the confines of its present culture, the nation ever seeks to purge itself of its color hate, it will find itself at war with itself, convulsed by a spasm of emotional and moral confusion. . . . Our America is frightened of fact, of history, of processes, of necessity. It hugs the easy way of damning those who it cannot understand, of excluding those who look different, and it salves its conscience with a self-draped cloak of righteousness. (272)

My guess is that what Wright is trying to tell us is that despite the observable corruption, America would like always to be perceived as a land of righteous whiteness, a world of achieved innocence. Our nation does not relish honest talk from blacks who have seen the corruption in the kitchen.

Wright's observations on the racial ideology of American culture, as well as his dilemma about raising a responsible hue and cry against corruption and evil, seem as meaningful in the 1990s as they were in the 1940s when *Black Boy* was published. Much of what Wright observes has to do with a continuous dynamics of *liking.* Where black men and women are concerned, there has always been a correlation between the narrator's, speaker's, or storyteller's "likableness" and the credibility assigned by whites to his or her tale. Wright seems certain, for example, that a "Negro girl" has a better chance of gaining a hearing than a "black boy." But he also clearly understands that if white men and women don't like your looks—a very substantial possibility in the case of "black boys"—they will not even listen to what you have to say. These white men and women, in fact, will almost never admit that yours is a significant and productive voice, important to the well-being of the nation.

Here, matters grow exceedingly tough. For what constitutes a likable black boy in the world Wright inhabits? In *Black Boy*, he gives stunning portraits such as the following:

> The most colorful of the Negro boys on the job was Shorty, the
> round, yellow, fat elevator operator. He had tiny, beady eyes
> that looked out between rolls of flesh with a hard but humorous
> stare. . . . "I'll do anything for a quarter," Shorty sang.
>
> "What, for example?" the white man asked.
>
> Shorty giggled, swung around, bent over, and poked out his
> broad, fleshy ass.
>
> "You can kick me for a quarter," he sang, looking impishly at
> the white man out of the corners of his eyes.
>
> The white man laughed softly, jingled some coins in his pocket,
> took out one and thumped it to the floor. Shorty stooped to pick it
> up and the white man bared his teeth and swung his foot into
> Shorty's rump with all the strength of his body. (227–28)

Shorty is likable. As is Griggs, who "when he laughed, covered his mouth with his hand and bent at the knees, a gesture which was unconsciously meant to conceal his excessive joy in the presence of whites" (185). We can be certain neither Griggs nor Shorty would hasten to tell stories about white corruption in the kitchen—or talk openly about the white American desire to exclude blacks from American culture altogether.

The silence of Shorty, Griggs, and their ever-with-us kindred on such matters—in combination with their ample willingness to do anything for a quarter—is what makes them eternally likable. Black affability is grotesquely profitable for selective likable blacks. But the desire of such blacks to be liked leaves awful facts of America untold, unheard, unanalyzed. And when such facts remain unarticulated, the process of *clearance*—exclusion or removal of blacks from rights, spaces, and privileges of American citizenship—goes forward with unchecked vigor.

With the help of Richard Wright and others, I now understand the inseparability of race, clearance, and liking, as well as nuances of American financing and promotion of black intellectuals. Wright grasped this inseparability as early as his first encounters with a bleak southern racism in Mississippi. He determined in the face of such bleakness to secure the means and nourish a black will to understand and critique conditions of global existence in ways that would not make him liked. He literally stole literacy from a Jim Crow system engineered not to nurture black dreams of citizenship, but to kill both the dream and the potential black citizen. We think of him battling both the black principal of his secondary school and all members of his immediate family in order to deliver the style and content of the speech he himself drafted for his eighth-grade graduation. We think of his story of forging a note over a white man's signature in order to secure books from a Memphis library: "Please let this nigger boy have some books by H. L. Mencken" (246). Wright's stolen literacy— by which I mean his radically secular and critical structure of feeling gained from reading and writing—produced a desperate hunger for politically engaged, in-depth, honest black talk as a *weapon* against southern ethics of living Jim Crow and a northern sociology and politics of black ghetto impoverishment. When Wright gained an audience, his path and mission as a black intellectual seldom varied. His was a habit of social critique. His mastery of American dynamics of race and understanding of race's myriad global valences make it impossible to ignore his intellectual integrity or the courageous magnitude of his critical legacy. However, later in life, Wright grew financially hard pressed; his access to a "general audience" became increasingly limited. His hard-edged candor became difficult not only for McCarthyite America to tolerate but also for neocolonial African readers to bear. We recall the near-hysterical African response to Wright's account of Ghanaian independence titled *Black Power*.

In later years of his career, one charge frequently leveled against Wright was that he was old-fashioned, out of date, and clinging (even in content and style) to the memory of a Jim Crow ethics his critics insisted had passed from the American scene forever. In a sense, this charge of *datedness* implies that memory—and particularly "racial" memory—forestalls modernity. What I would suggest, however, is that Wright's astute awareness of interconnections among race, power, economics, urbanity, and technology in the United States (an understanding conditioned precisely by his southern *racial* memory and his own brand of Marxist analysis) enabled him to join a global company of thinkers intent on achieving black, global, empowering modernity.

Wright can be viewed as a black person not simply hurt, outraged, and terrified by U.S. racism but also as a courageous black intellectual—a man memorially informed by racial wisdom he acquired during life under southern Jim Crow and northern red-lining and racist political assaults. From the vantage of our turn-of-the-millennium moment, it seems ironic that the black intellectuals promoted during the 1950s by American literary economics and prestige to displace Wright were certainly likable men. They commanded more conventional literary elegance than Wright. But they were also strikingly parochial in their understanding, representation, and relationship to southern black American life.

Of the novelist Ralph Ellison's relationship to the South, the black political scientist Jerry Gafio Watts writes:

> When reading Ellison's perceptions of the South one must remember that he did not experience the South from the vantage point of a native black southerner. Ellison's sense of possibility was decidedly that of a black raised outside the Deep South. . . . Ellison only experienced the periphery of southern black life during the age of Jim Crow. . . . Who but Ellison would have argued that attendance at a southern black college, life in a college town, and journeys to the countryside with the Tuskegee band would substantively immerse him in black life in the Deep South?[2]

And writing of the black essayist James Baldwin's journey of self-discovery and activism to the American South, the critic Daryl C. Dance observes: "His trip South so unnerved Baldwin that when he returned to New York, he collapsed, evidently suffering neurasthenia, or what he described as a paralysis resulting from retrospective terror."[3] The irony of Wright's American displacement is heightened, I think, if we acknowledge that neither Ralph Ellison (of whom I shall have more to say later) nor James Baldwin possessed a fraction of Wright's intelligence with respect to the dynamics of an unfolding world of postcolonial colored people.

Black modernity as elegant likability is a panorama altogether different, I believe, from such modernity conceived as a black critical memory that refuses to relinquish its racial roots. I believe critical memory compels the black intellectual such as Wright to keep before his eyes (and the eyes of the United States) a history that is embarrassing, macabre, and always bizarre with respect to race. The clarity bestowed by black critical memory is painful. It is terrible lucidity, casting dark light on a deeply troubling racial idea.

"Idea" is the proper word here. For race has always more to do, at least in the United States, with a nest of images, fears, envies, fantasies, and anxieties than with the root life or everyday comings and goings of real people. Which doesn't mean we can or should put "race" in quotation marks, as though it is a burst of sound from distraught social scientists. Race is still the ruling idea that conjures and pronounces sentences of guilt or innocence, life or death, acceptance or denial on we who are *black by choice* . . . or due to inescapable circumstance.

This sentencing of blacks—the spaces, stereotypes, manipulations, denials, and punishments we are subject to—is always full of meaning and consequences for the majority of America's citizens. This has been especially true during the past forty years of our national life. If ideas are America's most dangerous game, then the idea of race is the extreme sport of the past four decades— from the presidencies of John F. Kennedy to Richard Nixon, Ronald Reagan, and George Bush to the White House of William Jefferson and Hillary Rodham Clinton. Activist black intellectuals—those who bring black critical memory to bear on the idea of race—should receive triple hazard pay. What they are more apt to receive, however, is only the certain knowledge that their reports from memory (and still the "kitchen") make them too painfully real for whites to like. My personal journey from American southern youth to the present meditation has yielded strange dividends of clarity and distress that I hope readers will allow me a moment to explain.

I grew up in a segregated city on the banks of the Ohio River—a whiskey-distilling, baseball bat–manufacturing town—and spent youthful moments pondering what whites were thinking about me. Did they believe I was ugly, stupid, clumsy . . . a burden or a boon to my race? Since white people lived elsewhere and we rarely encountered them, it was almost impossible to get a responsible reading on their bodies, much less their minds. So my brothers and I relied on the wisdom of elders, fathers, aunts, uncles—those who had returned like scouts from alien territory.

Frequently our father would arrest a meal with the phrase: "Now that's just like the white man!" Sometimes we hadn't a clue what produced his utterance, though on other occasions our grandfather's or mother's reference to some item in the local newspaper seemed to be the trigger. With the words "Now that's just like the white man!" we knew our household's highest invocation of the racial muse had sounded. The moment was at hand to prepare for enlightenment—some news from the far country of colorless people (for we were known then as "colored") who existed elsewhere. Our dad's body would grow taut with wisdom:

"The white man is *trained* to believe he is superior. He does it by showing us as inferior. He has done everything, and I mean everything, in his power to keep us down, make us poor and stupid. Then he turns around and actually pretends to *show* us as stupid. Look at his cartoons; movies; the jokes he tells; names he uses for us. 'Nigger,' 'boy,' 'girl,' 'sambo.' Even his stories of us make *him* feel good. He makes us look like apes. He pictures himself as God Almighty! He makes us seem like monkeys, and then has the nerve to call himself *human*. Now you can't tell me that any. . ."

Our mother's gentle remonstrance would fall across our father's chant of demons. "Now, dear," she would say, "the children are trying to eat their breakfast." My father's coda to such epic outbursts involved looking sternly in mine and my brothers' eyes and instructing us: "Just remember, you're as good as any white man!"

The missing information was: How "good" could any man be who was vain enough to think himself God and cruel enough to depict us as monkeys, apes, or abysmally stupid "sambos"? Also, could it be true that all white people who lived elsewhere shared a single mind? Specifically, was it possible they all thought of me as ape, monkey, or "nigger"? In our isolated part of town, careful feedback on these matters was not always available.

On a late-spring Louisville Saturday afternoon, my father and I waited for an hour in the posh offices of a white orthodontist. Now surely it goes without saying there were very few black dentists in Louisville in the early 1950s; there were no black orthodontists. Moreover, the regnant wisdom among many blacks in my world on the Ohio was that black doctors were not as well trained as their white counterparts. Perhaps no media show was more aggressive in reinforcing notions of shysterish, poorly trained, buffoonish black "professionals" than *Amos and Andy*, which, sad to report, blacks did devour with the relish they brought to *Cosby* fantasies of the 1980s. There was thus more than one reason for my father's arrangements with the white orthodontist.

I must have been eleven or twelve years old that spring, because the book I carried somehow impressed my dad. It was not a little boy's book, but serious reading like *The Hardy Boys*. We waited and tried to be invisible. Cheery white mothers and their offspring said happy hellos and good-byes to the orthodontist. He didn't acknowledge our presence at all. We could have been a familiar old couch tucked in a far corner of the waiting room.

Finally, the office was quiet and empty. The receptionist—who had barely looked up when we entered—departed without so much as a nod. We sat, waiting. Half an hour passed before he summoned us into his examining room. The room had a cool, bright, circular white light focused on a dark green dental chair.

I climbed into the chair while my father stood watch. After a cursory exam, a few probes and grunts, he was finished. I knew, from the bathroom mirror, that my mouth was a mess of crooked front teeth, incisors that looked like warriors' spears, a jumble of recent and unnecessary molars, and a profound overbite that Bucky Beaver would have envied. After washing his hands thoroughly, Dr. Roberts turned to my father—who was dressed in the suit and tie he wore on all important occasions—and said: "There's nothing wrong with the boy's mouth that time won't take care of." My father was baffled, and stuttered: "But, but, but . . . what, what . . . ?" The orthodontist cut him off in midsentence: "Yes, I know, I know. It seems he'll always look like this. But that's because he has thick lips. If he exercises his upper lip by dragging his bottom front teeth over it, he can thin that lip and cover the crooked teeth. And his mouth in a couple of years will grow big enough to take care of the rest. Just thin the lip."

Then—as if some alien spirit imagined by Stephen Spielberg and filmed at Industrial Light and Magic had possessed him—his eyes rolled up. He began animatedly biting, scraping and chewing at his upper lip, mumbling all the while: "Can you see vat 'm doin'? He can do it jus like zis!" He had transformed before our eyes into a wildly distorted cubist portrait in the white light of the examining room. He kept mumbling through bites and scrapes of his teeth: "It's kinda like monkeys, you know? Only zay exercise ze lower lip." He was visibly drooling and gagging. But his last revelation about the monkey caused the possessive spirit to leave his body. He became again an orthodontist whose office was posh, and in the white part of town. I could barely breathe. I wanted to get out of that dark green chair and escape this man's ideas about my mouth . . . about me . . . about my father.

I know that Louisville afternoon was only one of a thousand warehoused memories that have led me to understand something about racial ideas and the "likability quotient" of blacks in the United States. Clearly, there was in that white man's mind an *idea* of me. And that idea produced both his nearly criminal professional opinion and his monkey-toothed, eyeball-rolling antics. His was a racialist medical diagnostic I am sure he never pronounced on whites. Certainly not on those cheery critters I peeked over my *Hardy Boys* book to see. He had only agreed to examine me in the first place because my father was superintendent of Louisville's Negro hospital and had made an appeal to his "professional courtesy." Even so, we were permitted to show up only after his weekend hours were to have ended. Normally, he never saw Negroes. Like me, he lived somewhere other than an interracial zone.

I was too shocked to entertain the notion that my dad should have punched the orthodontist's lights out. I now realize, of course, that my dad was also in shock. Actually, he must have been even more undone and humiliated since he was the father. Yet, curious to report, my dad sometimes commanded me over the next year to do my "lip exercise." This act of thinning becomes lodged. Keep *thinning*. Funny how such small instants can reveal the underbelly of a nation's most horrifying ideas. When such ideas are *racial*, they commence in America with the notion, fantasy, and conviction that black is the very color of malformation—an animalistic, maloccluded, unbearable ugliness.

Add *maleness* to black and the idea expands to include both excess (Why are you burdening the earth with your presence?) and *danger*. The great statesman Thomas Jefferson identified this danger. He located it in black memory. In his *Notes on the State of Virginia*, Jefferson avers that if white people decide to free blacks held in a profitable bondage, they must never allow them to remain on American soil. Why? Because, says Jefferson, the *memory* blacks possess of their treatment at the hands of whites will propel them into millennial warfare against their former enslavers. He prophesies that such warfare will conclude only with the extermination of one race or the other.

As I shaped the pages and reflections that follow I realized that *critical memory*—that and almost that alone—has always conditioned black Americans' likability and danger quotients in the mental life of white America. Now, this realization carries its own melancholy weight. For in sometimes sad, complicitous, self-destructive ways, we have assumed that if we blacks simply step back and erase our memory we will be allowed to remain healthily on American soil—and even be liked. On occasion, we have even dared to hope a self-directed erasure of our critical memory will enable us to join whites in defining the very word "like." Here, I mean "like" as a preposition. [*Like: prep., possessing the characteristics of; resembling closely; similar to.*]

But, if we return to that strange orthodontist of my youth, we know his guiding racial idea was that my father and I were very much unlike him. His American racial grammar was completely bereft of prepositions that might draw blacks in general, and certainly my father and I in particular, remotely close to him. For the orthodontist of a Louisville afternoon—as for Mr. Jefferson of Monticello in Virginia—"like" could only be a verb, one whose active possibilities and privileges were confined to whites. [*Like: v., to find pleasant; enjoy; to feel an attraction, tenderness, or affection for; to be fond of.*]

During my youth far too much black psychological, emotional, and intellectual energy was expended on the burden of white verbal privilege. I, and blacks in Louisville's isolated world around me, wanted whites to find us pleasant and enjoyable—sometimes more, in fact, than we seemed to want them *to join us* in a prepositional equality of resources and opportunities. There were, however, significant exceptions to expending black energy and talk on cosmetic attempts to be liked by whites.

Even though my father sometimes urged on my lip-thinning exercises, he nonetheless knew the value of critical memory for black people. Like Richard Wright, he had experienced the outrages and inadequacies of American racial ideas. Such injustices and inequities—actual harms to blacks at the core of American national life—conditioned his memory and taught him the necessity of translating memory's stores into clear cultural capital for black modernity.

The year was 1943. Spring was unusually cold on the Ohio. Having driven a battered secondhand car at dangerously high speeds to the colored institution called Red Cross Hospital because my mother was in labor with her second child, my father arrived to find only one sleepy nurse on duty. The building was cold and dark as Arctic winter. A failure of communication had left the white obstetrician uninformed that her presence was required. (There were, of course, no professional black obstetricians or gynecologists in Louisville.) Somehow my father got my mother into the hands of the nurse, found his way to the basement of the building to try and start the broken furnace, and failing to do so, had an electric heater put in her room, made contact with the obstetrician, called a furnace repairman, and then stopped in (briefly) to see his second-born son on the way to his "real job" as a teacher of commercial courses at Louisville's segregated Central High School.

Only thus was I born into a reasonably warm—though inadequately staffed and appointed—black hospital in 1943.

My father's memory of inadequacy and danger—as both he and my mother have told the tale—led him several seasons later to assume the post of superintendent of Red Cross Hospital. When he began, the place was no more than a cramped three-story brick house, with scarcely enough beds for even a modest patient load. Within three years of assuming the post, he launched a fund-raising campaign to construct a modern medical wing for the original structure. He needed a million dollars—an extraordinary sum of money in the late 1940s and, for some of us, in the 1990s.

My mother was co-lieutenant of the campaign. She was speech writer and financial consultant. As such, she continued a legacy of black womanist activism as critical for memorial offices of black modernity as any deeds of black men.

We recall, as case in point, the financial and emotional support provided by Ms. Anna Murray of Baltimore to the slave Frederick who left the South on Ms. Murray's largesse without so much as a last name. Frederick *Douglass* had no free beginnings without Anna Murray. We recall as well the black public-sphere and turn-of-the-nineteenth-century labors of the indomitable crusader for American justice Ida B. Wells. Of her traveling work for the Memphis-based newspaper *Free Speech*, which she edited, Wells writes:

> Being a native of the state [of Mississippi], which had been the strongest political organization in the South, I was handed from town to town from Memphis to Natchez . . . and treated like a

queen. I attended the [black] political meetings and church conventions besides the state bar associations and the Masonic grand lodge of the state, which suspended its labor to let me make an appeal for my paper. I was the daughter of Mississippi and my father had been a master Mason, so it was no wonder that I came out of the meeting with paid subscriptions from every delegate.[4]

Wells moved within the institutions of the black southern world with an ever-attentive memory and imagination. She was never reluctant to denounce injustice or to challenge black orthodoxies such as those of Booker T. Washington. When she brought scathing criticism to bear on the lynching of black men by southern whites, her newspaper offices in Memphis were burned.

In Louisville during the late 1940s, my mother continued a long-established tradition. She and Wells would have made a perfect combination. She went to private corporate institutions in search of funds for Red Cross Hospital. She successfully solicited Louisville's public utilities companies. Her most impressive work, like that of Wells and other forebears, was among conventions, churches, and political meetings of black Louisville. Everything was a contribution to the cause. My mother and black women who joined her in the campaign leased a small office in which to draft flyers and appeals. They counted and tallied endless dimes, nickels, pennies, and quarters that came from black folks. The goal was a black "peoples" institution.

Slowly the campaign gained recognition, resulting in a handsome editorial in the nationally recognized *Courier Journal*. My mother's speeches and my father's delivery of those speeches were working wonders. Suddenly, there was white philanthropy in the form of a matching grant from a businessman. The campaign succeeded. The Henry Heyburn Building—a new and modern wing of Red Cross Hospital—was dedicated on a bright, proud southern Sunday afternoon in the 1950s.

A memory that is *critical* not only hurts and outrages but also produces critique, strategic collaboration, intervention, and public-sphere institutions such as Ida B. Wells's newspaper for the people, *Free Speech*, and Louisville's Henry Heyburn Building. This I learned at home, in the house of my mother and father.

If we blacks in Louisville would never be "like" whites, we really did not let that stop us. For, we could and did set out our own definitions of what was "likely." [*Likely: adj., logically or expectedly about to occur; imminent.*] The example of my father and mother —along with that of ministers of black churches, black women teachers and librarians, black men and women civil rights advocates, and leaders of boycotts and sit-ins—were promises of imminence. Activist, re-membering black men and women showed us that good and indisputably *likable* things can come out of black life, if one remembers judiciously . . . shapes, ideas, and visions of what is likely, logically expected, and about to occur.

Like Richard Wright, my father and mother understood that literacy is the first servant of critical memory. She taught us the joy of words from Chaucer to Langston Hughes, reciting verses in lyrical bursts of self-confident smartness that gave us a model of creative address to life. He shaped a financial scheme whereby my brothers and I were rewarded with a dime for every book we checked out of the colored library and read. If we wrote reports on those wide-lined pads he bought for us, we earned a quarter. (Ours was, I think, a far more desirable way to earn quarters than Shorty's.) So, my older brother and I became something like manifestations of the *likely* as we worked the Henry Heyburn Building on our paper route, selling our town's African American weekly, *The Louisville Defender*, and checked out armloads of library books to read and review.

Critical memory produces not only public structures but also possibilities for the passage of black memory to a literate following of sons and daughters . . . who are us.

With critical care, the passage of black memory brings before our nation's eyes, in the phrasing of Mr. Jefferson, at least "ten thousand recollections" of what can occur when a powerful, rich elite assaults the rights of black men and women with impunity. At best, such impunity produces grotesquerie like the orthodontist. At worst, when black critical memory is under strenuous assault and silencing, the American majority—of all hues, religions, conditions, and geographies—suffers.

The work of critical memory, at the present time, is to lead the American majority to understand the real war against decency that has been waged against it, in the name of *race*, during the past forty years. This war has been propagated by a rich, white American minority, joined too often in its rhetoric and crimes against humanity by cadres of black neoconservative and centrist footsoldiers. The difference critical memory can make depends in large measure on the honesty of *black intellectuals* who are not seeking to be liked. The profit to be gained from honest, memorial labors of activist black intellectuals are, I think, benefits of a good life for *all*.

Failed Memory

Black Majority Modernism and Mr. Ellison's Invisible Man

Dear Irving [Howe], I am still yakking on and there's many a thousand gone, but I assure you that no Negroes are beating down my door, putting pressure on me to join the Negro Freedom Movement, for the simple reason that they realize that I am enlisted for the duration. Such pressure is coming only from a few disinterested "military advisers," since Negroes want no more fairly articulate would-be Negro leaders cluttering up the airways. For, you see, my Negro friends recognize a certain division of labor among the members of the tribe. Their demands, like that of many whites, are that I publish more novels—and here I am remiss and vulnerable perhaps.

—Ralph Ellison, "The World and The Jug"

We see in the merely exemplary instances of the Red Cross Hospital and Wells's *Free Speech* public-sphere examples of the positive productivity of black critical memory. However, there are always in the United States stunning failures of black critical memory. Often such failures remain beyond well-publicized "minority" critique because American arbiters of power and taste have placed them off limits to critique. When whites have determined that a "failure of black memory" is too likable to criticize, market forces and arsenals of American media protectionism make black critique nearly impossible. Likability translates, for the black chosen one, as an exclusive right to speak for "the Negro." The black likable thus becomes that immemorial American paradox—colored as hell, but "just an American," suddenly beyond confines of race.

Mr. Wardell Connerly is one of the most *liked* black men in America. He is deemed a veritable icon of the "fair chance for all," a devoted enemy of "racial" preferment. Of course, if Mr. Connerly were white, he would be *invisible*, justly bearing the irony of that now-defunct American band as his moniker: "the average white band."

In very recent years, the genuinely talented black comedian Chris Rock has gone from black nobody from Bed-Stuy to what *Time* magazine deemed "the funniest man in America."[5] *Time*, though, felt it necessary to trot out the likable black culture critic Michael Eric Dyson to explain why Rock's sudden success—which came close upon the heels of a comedy routine distinguishing "good" blacks from "bad" blacks, or "niggers"—was not a failure of black memory but an act of American non–racially protective courage. Similarly, the multitalented and now-retired basketball genius Michael Jordan seems to remain beyond critique for his complicity in Nike's exploitation of foreign workers producing Air Jordan sneakers. Mr. Jordan is beyond critique presumably because he is "America's canniest basketball player." Not only does America continue to "like" Mike, but countless television refrains suggest America wants to "be like Mike!"

Perhaps black public figures are to white "liking" as black public figures' discourses are to what Wright called America's "self-draped cloak of righteousness." To leave undisturbed white America's fear of "fact . . . history . . . necessity," to reinforce its derogation of the black majority, is, for the black public figure, to gain a dubious American spotlight of likableness. And, in our own era of mega-billion-dollar mergers such as CBS and Viacom, to earn likableness is to earn far more than Shorty's quarters!

I want to suggest that what makes black public figures in the United States likable to arbiters of power and taste is precisely their failures of black critical memory. As a case in point, I summon once again the most globally recognized African American writer of the twentieth century, Ralph Waldo Ellison. The one novel Mr. Ellison published, *Invisible Man*, is by almost any imaginable standard an "American classic." We must move back in time in order to commence a critique of this work, steering carefully around the off-limit lions of white critical adulation.

In the early 1950s, a black southern public sphere was emerging that would inaugurate a cataclysmic rights revolution, altering the very course of U.S. history, influencing movements for liberation the world over. Dr. Martin Luther King Jr., Rosa Parks, Fannie Lou

Hamer, Ella Baker, John Lewis, Arthurine Lucy, legions of black youngsters on a "Children's Crusade," blacks and whites staffing a "Freedom Summer" out of southern terror—these emergent agents of American rights were inconceivable to the author of *Invisible Man*. Or, at least, there is no hint of their imminence in *Invisible Man*. The grassroots resistance and organization—the utter determination for "freedom now"—that were bedrock for the Civil Rights Movement in America make no appearance in *Invisible Man*. The novel provides only an accommodationist black folk populace brokered by the likes of Dr. Bledsoe into rank submissiveness before white Trustees.

And when *Invisible Man* directs its attention to the North, it is scarcely more prophetic. Which is not to say there are no rebellious hipsters, hustling cartmen named Wheatstraw, and bodacious chameleon Rhineharts in Ellison's northern imaginary. No, it is not that Ellison missed the futuristic black "underground" altogether. He simply failed, or refused, to inscribe the process of that underground transforming itself into a field of revolutionary energy that changed the ways of black American folk for all time.

What accounts for such silence? Why does Ellison fail to praise, champion, or flesh out the revolutionary potential of a black civil rights public sphere in the South, or to strongly portray a genuinely efficacious public field of Black Power advocacy in the North?

Fundamentally, Ellison's "politics of silence" with respect to these black public domains is, first, a product of his decision to "hibernate" during the harrowing days of McCarthyism. He was not comfortable or secure enough to run against the American grain during an age of blacklisting, deportation, and House Un-American Activities Committee interrogations. When the inquisition is in full effect, it may be better to pretend to be a bear (rather than a lion) in winter. Second, I believe Ellison sincerely believed in the ideals ardently preached by American business: industrial democracy as the be-all and end-all of global modernity.

Modern man, for Ellison, is man attuned to the rhythms of the machine, to the currents and undercurrents of a raceless industrial capitalism. Modern man speaks and listens on an exclusively urban frequency, ever aware of ideological fault lines and complexities that make social responsibility a vexed obligation in a newly bureaucratic state. Hence, Ellison shares the politics and vision of an imperialist modernity, one of American exceptionalism. There is no trace in *Invisible Man*, for example, of global competition. In keeping with the Cold War mania of his era, however, there are certainly hints in *Invisible Man* of a pesky pinko outside agitation with respect to the Brotherhood's circuits of influence. Ellison seems utterly convinced that American modernity will—in part presumably through the philosophical musings of unengaged, hibernating, First Amendment, black "thinker tinkers"—pull itself onto the raft of equal rights and stop lynching (literally and symbolically) black folks before another century has passed. In 1994, Jerry Gafio Watts wrote of Ellison's faith in industrial-democratic individualism and its resultant political and artistic consequences:

> During the past twenty (and perhaps thirty) years, Ellison has not publicly been part of any organized black intellectual effort to confront racist practices in American intellectual life. Other black intellectuals have asked him to use his enormous prestige in this effort, but to no avail. . . . Ellison did not physically relocate to another land [like Baldwin or Wright], but his disengaged intellectual style may have been a necessary form of psychological emigration from the overbearing commitments and physiological

demands that accompany a politically engaged black intellectual existence in America. Ellison's willingness and ability to create a world of healthy black adaptation to subjugation may be nothing less than an attempt to fashion an image of the world that morally legitimates his political disengagement. It is, perhaps, a guilt-reducing fiction. (111–13)

In some ways, the fictional naiveté of Ellison's protagonist is completely emblematic of what might be called the "presentist simplicity" of *Invisible Man*'s own endorsement of industrial, imperialist, xenophobic American mythmaking. Layer upon layer of allusion mark *Invisible Man*'s chapters. In combination with the novel's Homeric ambitiousness, these allusive layers serve finally to obscure rather than to prophesy the actual, engaged, advanced-guard, public-sphere effectiveness of American blacks already at work, bringing *real* inklings of democratic modernity to the United States.

Simply stated, Ellison believed *morality*, *equality*, and *responsibility* were affirmative notions. And so they are. But blacks, at the very moment of *Invisible Man*'s receipt of literary awards on startling occasions, were transforming affirmative notions into decisively affirmative *actions*—converting the shadow to the act of black liberation. A black majority was courageously putting body and soul on the line and constructing a sphere of American ethical publicity undreamed (or even subtly implied) by Ellison's promising American fictions. The black New York novelist was stonily silent on the possibilities of an altogether unexceptional America—a postindustrial, radically black public-sphere–conditioned America (or, better, *Americas*). He was no prophet, and where the black public sphere is concerned *Invisible Man* provides no greatly prophetic matter.

Ellison's novel is burdened by belief, overwhelmed by excessive literary smartness, afraid to breathe life into its potentially revolutionary *cartoons*. For that, finally, is what so many figures on Ellison's fictional landscape are: mere cartoons, ventriloquized in the name of a certain species of democratic eloquence. They carry no black agential weight that might threaten anything or anybody constituting—in the words of W. E. B. Du Bois—the best white public opinion in America. But, surely, since Ralph Waldo Ellison has influenced the intellectual strivings of so many American liberal spokesmen, the foregoing assessment of *Invisible Man* must seem like dark, heretical ingratitude. But I mean no disrespect. I think such critical judgments as I have made must be supported by the novel's own weight of evidence.

Where "industry" and its white captains are concerned, need we look farther than the Trustee Mr. Norton or the export mogul Mr. Emerson? On power as the product—both beneficent and terrible—of industrial machines, need we search beyond that southern campus road in *Invisible Man* "with its sloping and turning"?[6] On this road is the "black powerhouse with its engines droning earth-shaking rhythms in the dark, its windows red from the glow of the furnace" (34). This uncanny scene of industrial power's dominance over black life reprises itself in the "deep basement" of Lucius Brockway at the northern Liberty Paints factory (207). Here, machinery, furnaces, and gauges lead the protagonist to an earth-shaking encounter with mysteries of American industry and industrialists alike. The hero's awe is palpable: "It's tremendous. It [Liberty Paints] looks like a small city," he exclaims (197). And in this "small city," he undergoes a machine-tooled rebirth from an electronic gizmo that subjects him to industrial lobotomy. The vagaries of black American life in the North come to seem like one huge industrial accident. Any benefits of industry that trickle down to blacks seem like pure products of welfare capitalism at its American worst.

Ellison's utter faith in industrial democracy is, in part, a function of his dependence on the brilliant analysis of the transition of black America from folk consciousness to industrial participatory democracy that appears in Richard Wright's *12 Million Black Voices*. While it may be true that Ellison repudiated Wright as a literary ancestor, *Invisible Man*'s strong anxiety of influence seems, in our era, rather obvious. There simply is no insight with respect to black folk consciousness, black northern migration, or black urban-industrial existence in *Invisible Man* that is not anticipated in *12 Million Black Voices*. Listen to Wright: "In industry . . . we encounter experiences that tend to break down the structure of our folk characters and project us toward the vortex of modern urban life."[7]

Wright's narrative, however, understands that black factory work is merely a counter to white labor union initiatives. It is always contingent upon a power politics of racial exclusion. Though blacks may work cheaply for Western civilization, says Wright, they are never allowed to live equitably as citizens *within* Western civilization. Nevertheless, the Great Depression showed black and white workers their common class interests. The old black folk consciousness died an economically motivated death during the Great Depression. Barriers of race and class were transcended by a beleaguered proletariat. The "Bosses of the Buildings" trembled before a new communalism, if not an actual progressive communism. Modernity, for Wright—whose politics are completely alien to Ellison's philosophizing hibernation—is nonfolk, industrial, and interracially proletarian.

Indeed, for Wright, modernity is at its best when it is engaged in strict scientific scrutiny and *critique* of capitalism and its "bosses." Ellison's *Invisible Man* co-opts most of Wright's poetical insight about black modernity. But Ellison cartoonizes a flesh-and-blood black majority's everyday life as well as Wright's critique of capital. The author of *Invisible Man* pays little studied attention to the intimate horrors of racism in the United States. He relinquishes such analysis for an Eliotian or Hemingwayesque pottage of allusions. Wright works as an embattled, public, activist, black intellectual. Ellison writes as though intellectualdom is both colorblind and capable of effective, nonengaged, philosophical intervention in the terrors of race in these United States.

What locks Ellison so dramatically into a colorblind, literarily allusive prison of language is his novel's supposition that white policing and surveillance are utterly inescapable by black Americans. All black life in the United States, *Invisible Man* implies, is no more than a black battle royal. And black "territory" is no more than a zone of containment without remedy and impervious to critique. So why not simply hibernate until things change? Here is Ellison's protagonist on being led into a hotel ballroom for his first encounter with white discipline and punishment: "I was shocked to see some of the most important men of the town quite tipsy. They were all there—bankers, lawyers, judges, doctors, fire chiefs, teachers, merchants. Even one of the more fashionable pastors" (18). Of course, the ironic stupidity of the protagonist's "shock" is heightened because he is the "smartest kid in the class." Even the smartest blacks, Ellison implies, can't escape the professional white gaze. The protagonist believes he is being ushered into the ballroom to present, yet again, his high school valedictory address. After he is beaten severely by one of "his own," the hero stands bloody but unbowed in his American faith. He delivers his speech. It is about blacks staying faithfully in their containment areas. When he stumbles upon the phrase "social equality," he quickly retracts it under the immediate threat of white professionalism (31). The Invisible Man is no "native intellectual." He is, rather, the "native" as intellectual—an ersatz intellectual in the service of the white containment and *clearance* of black folks in America.

Like the factory and industrial power scene, this battle royal leitmotif reprises itself in *Invisible Man*. Its politics of containment are apparent in the white American woman stripper who is brought in by the "most important men of the town" to titillate white male fantasy and tempt bare-chested black boys. A voyeuristic white politics of bodily-sexual taboo and containment is contingent upon white women's reduction to sex objects and nothing more. Remember, it is at the hero's most effective moment of Harlem Brotherhood work that he is transferred from uptown to white downtown as an all-but-bare-chested orator on the "woman's question." He becomes a black stud for white power. The sad politics of black men's and white women's disempowerment in America acquire a new convert.

Ralph Waldo Ellison—the valedictorian of African American letters—reads the black public sphere as a white-instigated and controlled battle royal. His reading misses, of course, all the nascent energy of Civil Rights and Black Power. And when Civil Rights and Black Power became American—indeed global—realities, Ellison reclined in butter-soft seats at exclusive Manhattan clubs, explaining to whites why he could *not* take any active part in the liberation politics of black Americans. America's industrial, democratic, lobotomizing machine—like the sleep of reason—had produced a clubbable monster in Ellison. One is tempted to sample James Baldwin's postmortem of Richard Wright and say: "Alas, Poor Ralph!" He completely missed the *real* modernity of America.

But this, of course, is not the entire picture. Ellison was obsessed with the power of a white, industrial, bureaucratic state (see Peter Wheatstraw's fetishizing of those ever-changing "plans" of the Bosses of the Buildings [175]). His obsession forestalled effective prophesy for "tomorrow," but it did not prevent his "hearing around corners."

Invisible Man possesses a striking array of interlinear characters who make brief—sometimes cartoonlike—appearances and then are heard no more. Their tales, however, are not those of idiots signifying nothing. Quite the contrary. These interlinear characters are precisely the ones Ellison's fear of McCarthyism—and an obsessive phobia of not being liked—kept him from fleshing out. The interlinear possibilities of black, public, intellectual action par excellence I have in mind are Ras the Exhorter, Tod Clifton, Brother Tarp, Rhinehart, Mary Rambo, among others. They are potentially activist and engaged Fanonian native intellectuals; they offer potential for effective black leadership in *Invisible Man*. They have broken the manacles, dropped out of official history, learned the mastery of form, preserved and transformed the best of black folk consciousness, and are unbelievably *eloquent*. Brother Tarp is a model for Toni Morrison's Hi Man and Paul D in the novel *Beloved*. Everywhere—like a ticking black bomb in *Invisible Man*—there simmers a potential for effective black public-sphere leadership.

But the novel denies its own best insights by incarcerating all its interlinear figures in a Disneyesque prison of American novelistic form that declares: "No Efficacious Black Leaders Need Apply!" The white Trustees' panopticon overwhelms and terrifies Ellison's narrative into hiding its own best self. *Invisible Man* is asymptotic to that great curve of *actual* black life in America where leadership emerged on the world stage—full force—during the Civil Rights Movement.

The acclaim bestowed on *Invisible Man* was, at least in part, a function of the novel's cautious reassurance to white folk that black leadership was but an incarcerated-suppressed-*cleared-*

stifled-cartoonish-controlled epiphenomenon. Certainly, one reading effect of *Invisible Man* is a sense of security for white readers (or *power* in general). This effect stems from the seeming impossibility of a public-sphere effectiveness by black, activist intellectuals in America. After all, the old black woman who killed her master in the novel's prologue is a "dream vision" from the "old days." The protagonist himself is an underground talking head—in covert preparation like some Central Intelligence Agency mole—waiting for a better day a-comin' (13). Full of angst and poignant longings for democracy, his is an autobiographical tale of alienated black intellectualdom in a binary, strenuously policed universe of locked bodily positions: black man–white man, white woman–black man. There is scarcely a black woman who is given a chance to speak intelligently in Ellison's novel—a dutiful wife or an Amen-ing churchgoer is all the novelist can muster.

Ellison's protagonist is an end-of-ideology—even an end-of-history—existential intellectual, out of time, blackly ruminating. He is modeled on the brooding voices of Russian fiction and the conservative despair (but not the engaged and sardonic critique) of T. S. Eliot's *Waste Land*. The voices of protagonist and narrator constitute a veritable archive of white literary modernism. They are literarily "American" to a fault. The narrative's intention is clearly to be *the* Great American Novel . . . alas! And, wonder of wonders, it worked like a charm, indeed, brilliantly! For the panoramic, black-disempowering, white-reassuring view of race matters that *Invisible Man* offers is exactly what America always welcomes. *Here's Sambo, unselfconsciously on a Lambo, working to delight white folks!* (It is only *after* Tod Clifton's death that the protagonist discovers the "invisible string" Clifton used to *master* white expectations of eternal black entertainment.)

Ellison's stylistic risks and almost breathtaking leaps of story line are venturesome indeed. They warrant admission to PEN. Moreover, his novel's insights can dramatically inform and expose subtleties of race for American whites. But where in *Invisible Man* is the *actual* black future? Where is the future's effective public-sphere activism? Where is the free-improvisational, unbossed, and unbought autonomy that constitutes black agency? Where is the courage of nine black boys and girls braving white mobs to attend formerly segregated precincts of an Arkansas public school? Where are the white Americans, the Jewish Americans who gave up the comfort and security of the American racial status quo in order to help bring about a rights revolution in this land? Where are they, where are they in *Invisible Man*? They do not exist—even in potential—in Ellison's novel.

Even the Harlem riot of *Invisible Man* cannot escape the white Trustees' agency: it is explained as a calculated result of Brotherhood intelligence and policing. Damn! Even those extraordinarily *bad* brothers who won't steal a hat unless it is a Dobbs are, finally, reduced by Ralph Waldo Ellison to pawns of the Brotherhood. This indeed is black individual talent under sad and serious arrest. We weep, literally, for talent lost.

Where is the Black Future in Ellison's novel? Why do we have ganja and sloe gin and dreamy haziness as the atmospherics for the black intellectual's ultimate state of narration? And then there are blues—not of Memphis Minnie or Barbecue Bob—but of Louis Armstrong. "Pops" was America's great accommodationist goodwill ambassador to the world. (Which is not to deny that Satch was a musical genius!)

How, then, in the actual presence of Ellisonian silencings do we talk about the possibilities of a black public sphere that is free from the Trustees' gaze? Only by energizing—transforming through our own agency—Ellison's cartoons. Tod Clifton and Mary Rambo, Rhinehart and Brother Tarp are filled with black-boardinghouse, conjure-spiritualist, yam-selling, chameleon energy that is *not* to be feared—it is to be cultivated. These inter-linears are the garden where Alice Walker's narrator goes in search of liberating syllables. They are the grass roots of Civil Rights and Black Power.

Now why—with such an array of underground and black public-sphere possibilities—does *Invisible Man* exude pale, existential moderation as its politics? Why can't Ellison's protagonist assume his articulations from the adroit machinations of a sphere always already in motion? The novelist's silence on this count—his resistance to such potential—results from Ellison's belief that these underground black figures are either beneath or bereft of understanding. Underground potential is cartooned in the office of white entertainment. *Invisible Man* is ultimately—at far too many narrative moments—a novel of American local color in its comically basest minstrel manifestation. Had Ellison been genuinely invested in a black, public, activist intellectual enterprise with respect to his novel, the book's idiom would certainly have reflected the black underground far more astutely and pro-phetically than it does. The novel's ending—which, as we are told, is implicit in its beginning—would never have been a cozy, coy, tinkering intellectual hibernation pleasing to white folks.

Had Ellison seen prophetically and with great black, activist intellectual power the future orientation, uprootedness, and postmodern gesturing of his interlinear black *deponibles*, he would have breathed considerable novelistic life into them. He would not have missed so completely the black spirit of his times. He might even have joined James Baldwin in that black Parisian exile's historic journey back to what Ellison calls the "old coun-try" (the American South) to, at least, do something for the black majority even if he could not fully comprehend its spaces of habi-tation. Who knows? After such knowledge as Baldwin possessed of the "New Black South," Ellison might even have licensed himself to trim the allegorical layerings of his novel; he might have become less self-consciously and literarily "modern." Less a Hemingway and more blessedly a postmodern Langston Hughes, or, best of all, a true ancestral avatar of Richard Wright, who was not concerned to be liked by white bards and New York reviewers. But that journey of Ellison politically to the South never happened.

Instead Ralph Waldo Ellison became complicitous with writers clubs and *silence*. He fantasized a noncorrespondence between his own well-rewarded self and the black majority. For what *Invisible Man* implies about an immanent American racial morality and equality of citizenship for the majority of black Americans under the aegis of industrial democracy—or any other system of white American power—is pure poppycock! Ellison's "democratic" preachments are, as one of his own heroes, Huckleberry Finn, would have phrased it: soul-butter and hogwash. In fact, it is only the underground agency of Ellison's interlinear black figures that, in fact, propelled the United States toward a crisis of race matters during the 1950s and 1960s and bid fair to call our country to an honest account of its relationship to the black majority in the 1970s.

From an actual South that is unseen in *Invisible Man* to a North that is never given its due, a pulsating, flesh-and-blood (not allegorical) blackness-of-blackness transformed America and the world at large. Ellisonian interlinearity—the novelist's cartoons, as in some avant-garde leap of animation—became actively essentialist. They became embodied, in-motion, and concrete in ways that led to actual *rights* in America. Up from the underground they came. Out of the black hole of abjection they arose. They passed Ellison's *Invisible Man* as though the novel were Wile E. Coyote and they the New Age Mexican (existential "Native

American") Roadrunner. ZAP! They went so fast that Ellison believed them out of history. His narrator calls for the old industrial bridge to stay in place. The bridge is rational. The bridge is the Enlightenment. The bridge is the "Negro Intellectual as Smartest Kid in the Class." Here is individualism devoid of activist responsibility to a black majority, much less writerly responsibility for a scathing (à la Wright) *critique* of capitalism.

So Ellison's hero is spelunking in a well-lighted cave, listening to Louis Armstrong while smoking pot and drinking gin. Meanwhile, the black majority brings about a moral revolution that Ellison is unable to comprehend, unwilling to join. Ellison lived silently by the Hudson, dined at New York clubs, became an icon of what a black writer is when he turns the revolutionary potential of a black majority into a white-disciplined *cartoon*. No correspondence between Ellison and the black majority.

Now, of course, *Invisible Man* is satire, not photorealism designed for Marxist agitprop. But satirists who portray their protagonists as hapless misanthropes have been known to go mad. Witness Jonathan Swift. Perhaps the converse of madness is the paralyzed inability to get on with the next novel, or an uncharitable basking in the felt sense of one's own importance. Ellison sadly became a victim of his own satire. But this has not, alas, frightened away imitators, converts, disciples, avatars, and wanna-bees. That list includes Albert Murray, James Alan McPherson, Ernest Gaines, Charles Johnson, Al Young, and others. These black men have been second-order adherents to industrial democratic faith in the kindness, the social and economic goodwill, of white American strangers. Dedicating their work to the spirit of the "best white public opinion," unstintingly harsh in their damning of any creativity grounded in either the theories for understanding or the techniques and themes deriving from racial discourse, Charles Johnson and others produce musing, philosophical, entertaining, all-American, blackface minstrel romps . . . for money.

Normally commencing—like Ellison—with some classic model of American exceptionalism—some American sacral text—as their guide, books like *Middle Passage*, *A Gathering of Old Men*, and *Elbow Room* traipse blackly out to the territory and find that Negroes, too, can be misogynistic seafaring boors, vacuously unrepentant ninnies about a white overseer's death *if* they are under the protection of pretty white women, or lost in the funhouse of American identity crises if they work hard at *not* being black.

In a 1996 *New York Times Book Review* essay devoted to the recent work of Albert Murray, Charles Johnson wondered why more attention was not paid to Murray. The answer is that nobody really needs to pay any attention to Murray. His faith—and its attendant prescriptions and fictional spin offs—signal a disengaged politics of hibernation that constitutes the meanest, lowest form of individual self-interestedness. And what reader—black or white, Asian or Latino—with a multicultural view of the United States as part of the Americas cares one whit about Albert Murray's holed-up apologias for the xenophobic maxims and pretended goodwill of "democracy"?

On the other hand, who but those in search of a willful blindness to the complexities and possible public-sphere incumbencies of black writing in the United States would mistake Charles Johnson's fiction as anything other than a parody of a parody? Johnson hails Murray's parodic cartoonish vision of life as American revelation. But this is because Johnson himself, for money, has imitated the worst of both Ellison and Murray in the name of "art" and a "phenomenological" philosophical sophistication. The world of Ellisonian avatars is parody . . . all the way DOWN.

Ellison did—by all counts—have stylistic eloquence and remarkably powerful intellectual range. He was ambitious, and I think principled, in his refusal to participate in the liberational black future unfolding around him. He believed that art was the ship and all else the sea. But Ellison's "ghosts"—his shadowers—have not displayed august critical talent, sincerity, or even ambitiousness in their art. They have no capacity, it sometimes seems, for principled ethics. They have gladly accepted the affirmative action benefits and rewards bestowed by race in America while writing fiercely and with studied hypocrisy that there is no such thing in America as race.

Here's Sambo on the Lambo with no strings attached!

Philosophical or political rubrics such as "existential humanist" or "neoconservative contrarian" cannot excuse their self-interested feigning at *race transcendence*. Their hypocritical acceptance of dollar bills and prizes constitutes, finally, a pseudo-American Uriah Heepism that would have made Ellison heave. But this is not an essay about America's Nouveau Blackface Race Transcendentalists. Nevertheless, as Nick says about Gatsby at the end of Fitzgerald's American classic, Ellison was far better than the gang that has followed him.

Today, now—and ironically from the increasingly "Americas oriented" precincts of the elite university—I know I am a pure product of the energy and spirit that marked Harlem, 1964—a moment of black American intellectual activism in motion. Through the wisdom of the sometimes frantic and rambunctious 1960s, I began to learn to avoid the devastations of Jack the Bear as well as the evasion, cynicism, hibernation, and longings for safe passage of Rhinehart. Perhaps I learned from the sixties that there are no safe passages in America for activist black intellectuals. But if the realization that there are no safe passages has arrived, there is yet an even more salient revelation, and that is precisely that the *absence of safety* is metaphorical for us all, for the American majority. I ponder the fate of the National Endowment for the Humanities, of the National Endowment for the Arts, of *tenure as we know it*, of multicultural *difference* faced with a right-wing–financed homogenization threatening to compact us all, as Baldwin would phrase it, to the bloodless dimension of a guy named Joe. I think of the rigors of black activist intellectuals, and they seem to signal a lonely road ahead. Richard Wright returns as companion, however, in *12 Million Black Voices*, speaking the words of fathers and uncles as follows: *Look at us and know us and you will know yourselves, for we are you, looking back at you from the dark mirror of our lives!* (146).

Words of a black majority. Words for action. A metaphorical call from black fathers and uncles to the American majority about our nation's well-being. The fortunes of critical memory and critique reside in a capacity to step behind the rising minstrel action of American race transcendentalists such as Ellison, Shelby Steele, Murray, and others to catch a firm vision and more thoughtful sense of black intellectual obligation. Through critical memory we learn to look upon Ralph Ellison and his progeny "not as in the hour of thoughtless youth." For now the hour is late and our time limited. And only critical memory can summon to view and hearing the "still, sad" (but undeniably public, black majority, activist) "music of humanity." Issuing the call, stepping critically back, the metaphor and sounding of fathers and uncles demands committed intellectual response. This *is* the wisdom of Wright's mirror.

Words for Black Fathers and Sons in America

Symbolic Politics and a Million Man March

The black men who came to Washington to march on the Mall were younger, wealthier and better-educated than black Americans as a whole, and they were far more willing to see Nation of Islam leader Louis Farrakhan assume a more prominent leadership role in the African American community, according to a Washington Post poll of participants in the Million Man March.

—*Washington Post*, October 17, 1995

Whippersnapper clerks
Call us out of our name
We got to say mister
To spindling boys.

—Sterling Brown, *Old Lem*

I cannot accept that "balance the budget" will ultimately eclipse a concern to balance the distribution and availability of wealth, of chances for self-respecting survival.

—June Jordan, *Notes of a Barnard Dropout*

The bone-piercing cold, the rock salt on driveways, the bitter chill, the smell of grocery-store sawdust in midwinter. A gray light on gaunt, disfigured roofs. Such early memories from the Louisville where I grew up are sharpened, made more unpleasant, by the recalled absence of my father and the fear that it occasioned in me. During my youth, when my father was not at home in the evenings, I felt unprotected, vulnerable, afraid. When he was out of town, I was terrified, incomplete. And he was absent from us the entire winter of 1947–48.

He had seated himself at his desk—at work, of course, before 7:00 A.M.—one morning in 1947 and drafted a letter to the Rockefeller Foundation in New York. He told them about his efforts at Red Cross Hospital, suggesting that he needed to achieve a master's degree in hospital administration in order to do a proper job of health care for the Louisville Negro community. With uncommon speed the foundation replied, congratulating him on his labors and offering funds for the full costs of his graduate study. They informed him that Northwestern University had one of the premiere programs in hospital administration in the world. When winter came, my father was in Evanston, Illinois. He left Red Cross Hospital in the hands of Mrs. Hyatt, the chief nurse. He passed responsibility for the grocery store that he and my mother had purchased in a section of town called "Little Africa" to my mother. Said goodbye to his sons. And with as much ebullience as he could muster waved to us from a smeared train window.

That winter was desperately cold. Frost formed inside windows. We continuously shoveled coal into the one heat source in our tiny house—a bulky brown stove that licked flame each time we opened the door. (One day, my older brother and I played garbage man, shoving canceled checks from a box in our mother's bedroom into the flames. Before she spanked us with a switch, she cried for a long time.)

My father's absence in the isolation of winter made me physically ill. I came down with a cold that lasted weeks. Alone in the chill, empty house, with the gray light of winter through frosted windows, I grew tense at every creak and moan. I was miserable; I was afraid. My mother came home at noon to give me medicine . . . and Campbell's soup. During these noontime rituals her face was drawn and weary. She was frustrated with my illness, the grocery store's endless demands, the refusal of winter to break its frigid hold. My father was gone, and the only break in the somber rounds of his absence came when our uncles (my mother's brothers) visited.

They were men who seized virtual images of possible futures for themselves and their sons. Men who conjured in their waking hours undreamed opportunities. Men who believed they would some day assume a place at the American table, a space commensurate with their talents and education. And if not they, then certainly their sons would sit comfortably at the table, rightly rewarded.

Like my father, these uncles had left home bent on preparing themselves for summonses from the offices of the American meritocracy. "If we build ourselves justly and righteously, THEY will come to us!" Motto of my uncles. I think they sensed, during that bitter winter of 1947–48, that their sister—our mom—was a woman on the verge of a serious loss of faith in the American dream. They came to provide reinforcement.

When Uncle Gordon came, we knew we had to be on our best

behavior. He asked probing questions: How were we doing in school? How did we feel about our classmates? Were our teachers "professional"? What did we know about God and the Bible? Gordon was dour, sometimes self-centered to the point of a one-word response. He might simply grunt in response to our cheery "Hi" if he was reading one of the endless books, newspapers, and magazines he seemed always to have ready at hand.

Gordon told stories of his son Ashby. In his stories, young Ashby was always the winner—a brilliant turner of tides. Ashby was, in fact, not much older than my own brother. But when he visited us in Louisville, he seemed ancient, as full of encrypted wisdom as the hills or rivers. Ashby either wouldn't or didn't know how to play. He just sat in the swings and made up absurd country-and-western lyrics like: "Loaded pistols and loaded dice / Can make you feel / Like you're eating rice." Over and over . . . Ashby, the genius.

There was an entirely different rhythm to our Uncle Vance's visits. His voice and laughter were the closest incarnations of Jolly Old St. Nick I have ever encountered. He was not a particularly robust man, but he had a deep bass voice and a definite "Ho, Ho, Ho!" that made the house shake. His questions were easier to answer: What sports did we like? How did we think the Dodgers would do now that Jackie Robinson was part of the team? Which of us was the strongest, and would we like to arm wrestle with him? Vance's son, "Butch," (Vance Jr.) was definitely—at least in his father's account—not a genius. He was a colored Dennis the Menace. But Uncle Vance's daughters—of whom there were two—were certifiably MENSA (they literally knew everything). According to Vance, Butch was "full of the devil" and "too clever for his own good." You saw Vance's chest puffing out, buttons straining, even as he tried to look conscientiously disturbed about the devilish propensities of his son. When Butch came to visit, we had one of the most exciting, imaginative, on-the-edge summers I can remember. Butch always had worlds of projects in his brain: turning the upper room of our decrepit garage into a "Victory Club," beating up the little white boys around the corner who would shout after us "Nigger, nigger pull the trigger / Up and down the Ohio River / Snotty nose and dirty clothes / That's the way a nigger goes." My brother and Butch rode off one day on bikes and beat the living daylights out of those twin white chanters, whose parents had imaginatively named them Ronny and Donny.

Then there were visits by Uncle Webster. He brought along with him on one occasion a puppy—brown and black, German Shepherd, cute. Since the puppy was more black than brown, my brother and I named him Blacky. "No, indeed!" said our father on one of his trips home from Northwestern, "You can't name him that." Why? Well, our father explained: "Suppose you were calling the dog and someone in the grocery store thought you were talking to them?" "Blacky" became "Shep." Webster had no children. But I believe he looked upon me and my two brothers, always, as his sons.

In the winter of 1947–48, snow accumulated, ice was everywhere, cold drafts stole in at window sills, and frigid air burst into the living room each day when my brother returned from Virginia Avenue Elementary School. And then winter was gone. Bright, warm sunshine thawed the southern ground, and Grace Presbyterian Church got ready for Women's Day and Easter Sunday services. My brother and I traveled with our mom to Chicago, stayed with Uncle Gordon and Aunt Melba, and attended our father's commencement ceremony at Northwestern University. I remember my father as pale and thin in his black graduation gown. Most of all I remember the ranks of dark-uniformed, newly trained police rookies who had just completed a law-enforcement degree. My father took me up in his arms that afternoon and kissed me on the cheek and thanked me for "helping Mom through the winter." I could have been atop the highest, safest mountain in the world in that man's arms on that afternoon. Still, the entire day was strange—too full, like a frightened heart with pent-up emotion. That night, I wet the bed. A whole winter had passed, and nothing like that had happened. What was wrong? What unknown marker had shifted out of place? My Aunt Melba said: "You should be ashamed of yourself. A big boy like you!" But I didn't feel big, only safe, for the moment. Because I knew my father and uncles—and even my brother, who was eerily kind to me on that trip—would protect me. My Daddy, after all, was a "Masters of Hospital 'Ministration."

My uncles—like my father—died too early. In some ways, I believe it was the agony, illness, turmoil, and still-barricaded roads that beset their sons that took their lives. My cousin Ashby, at age thirty-three, awakened one night with fever, shortness of breath, pain. The doctors said it was a mysterious virus; they could find no way of treating it. Ashby died within a month. My Uncle Gordon—as though in holy communion with his son—died of the same "mysterious virus" within months. Our cousin Butch was examined by a Coast Guard surgeon on a Monday prior to shipping out on assignment. The surgeon pronounced Butch completely fit. The following Wednesday, as he was walking up the gangplank to his command, Butch died of a heart attack at age thirty. Uncle Vance lost his laugh. Age lines crept under his eyes. He became dour.

Our father sprinted into the 1950s with his Northwestern master's degree. He transformed Red Cross Hospital into an impressively modern facility. Then, full of *Brown v. Board of Education* enthusiasm, he was forced to listen and, one suspects, tremble as my older brother marched, sat in, picketed, and got soundly beat up by southern racism. (Which, of course, is merely Western Hemispheric racism with a Confederate flag.) My mother was terrified for my brother's safety, and my father said: "Well, I hope he understands those white crackers will beat his head and not bat an eye!" Our parents worried my brother out of the South. He came north and entered law school.

In the 1950s, our father negotiated the nonviolent direct-action dangers of his oldest son. He abided my obsessive-compulsive studiousness, neuroticism, paranoia, and fears produced by integrated education in Louisville. He also worked earnestly to understand the socialization difficulties of elementary education (that is, newly integrated elementary education) of his youngest son. Why were *his* sons almost as hard pressed and encumbered by American racial dynamics as he had been? Hadn't he worked hard enough? Where was the call from the Offices of American Meritocracy? Our father tried moving to Washington, D.C., seeking a larger field of health care work at the old Freedmen's Hospital. But it was not a good time for a family move. So, back he came to Louisville—with a lower-paying personnel job in the Mammoth Insurance Company. Our father was a man of ambition, possessing an almost heroic capacity for long, disciplined hours of work. But his sons seemed in turmoil. American life would not unfold according to his best expectations of integration or the virtuality that had driven him through a Wharton School MBA and a wintry Northwestern graduate career.

I know it was the toll of unfulfilled promises, the dangerous closed roads for his sons, that hastened the cancer that traveled through my father's bones, ate cells of his marrow. My father died too young.

Our Uncle Webster—despite the incoherent speech and indecipherable handwriting that frightened his friends in Barcelona—refused to admit that he needed medical attention. His life had been exceedingly troubled by New York City School Board politics during 1986–87. Race was playing an increasingly critical role in the public schools where he was a supervisor. A black and Hispanic majority was becoming the norm. Webster's stroke came full-blown, dropping him to the ornate bricks of his Barcelona hotel room patio. When my older brother and I arrived at the hospital fronting the sea in Barcelona where he had been admitted, he could only groan, flail his arms . . . tears flowed without stopping. He died a year later in a Brooklyn facility.

Fathers and sons. The dynamics of black men dreaming in the United States. The garnering by black men of educational resources. Their grasp and understanding of the calculus of American racial "likes." None of the men from my growing-up time got rich, famous . . . or secured their sons' futures. Their integrity remained strong; they worked wherever and whenever they could to hasten the call and reality of a reported American meritocracy —a meritocracy renovated, or so one was told, in the 1950s and 1960s by *Brown v. Board*, Civil Rights, the War on Poverty, and pronouncements of goodwill and a New Frontier by white men in charge of the American table.

From the obituary of my father that appeared in the *Washington Post* on Tuesday, December 6, 1983, comes the following testimony of his American faith: "Mr. Baker was a president of the Association of Assistant Administrators of Hospitals of the National Capital Area, the chairman of the D.C. Board of Examiners for Nursing Home Administrators, a director of the 12th Street YMCA and the Health and Welfare Council of Washington, and chairman of the education advisory council of the D.C. Board of Education."

All the black men of my growing-up time looked, at one moment or another, into their sons' lives and struggles—into their sons' very eyes—and saw that their sons' notions of the present and future were perhaps even bleaker than theirs had ever been.

And they saw, in that moment, the unbearable. Their boys' racial existence in America was going to be as inescapably burdensome as their own. And then there were the sons' deaths—Ashby and Butch—presumed genius and devil, respectively.

Black men die in the United States of overwork, failed hopes, their sons' absence, and the realization that their children's somber explanations and expectations of life are almost certainly accurate forecasts of the future. Black men die early and often because almost nothing ever alters in America with respect to race. Not only does the spitting in the food in the kitchen continue, but now those in power are energetically *clearing* away from the American table millions of children simply to starve. In the late 1990s, final decade of a century that has promised much and delivered little for black Americans by way of equal *status* with a white majority, the starvation of children was called welfare reform, and it was overseen from the presidential White House. Corrupted food is one thing; starvation is altogether another.

Black fathers and sons in America grow distraught, glimpse a torturous future, perish at too-early ages. I have watched the black men in my family disappear under the onslaught of racial politics and entailments in the United States. And I stand in sad and respectful witness now to what so many black fathers in America have known. I know, today, that the old gospel song does not apply to my own son's life. He cannot sing: *It is well, it is well, it is well with my soul!*

The black men in my family died of too much hope, perished from the absence of opportunities. The black men who have disappeared from my family could not save themselves or their sons in all too many instances. But, I—and so many others like me—have refused to stand in mute witness to the deaths of our fathers, uncles, cousins, friends, and brothers at the hands of American secrets and lies . . . but by now, you are surely asking: "Have the mothers, sisters, daughters, nieces no part in all of this?" And the answer is, of course they do.

In the cold, frightening time of my father's absence, our mother fought winter, fueled the brown stove, kept us and the business of the grocery store alive . . . showed us she loved us. Explained to us in a steady slow voice *why* our father had to secure a master's degree in hospital administration. Her nights were spent alone in a bedroom no warmer than our own. We were never hungry, shunted aside, or refused help or counsel on any of the worries of black southern childhood. And our mother watched our father die much too soon.

She knows now, in her nineties, what she knew in the winter of 1947–48: that it is as much black men's hopes for their sons, in combination with broken democratic promises of America, that kill black men early and too often. And our mother resolutely joined other mothers and daughters and sisters on a fall day not so long ago to watch (and, for all I know, *pray*) as those of us who have refused to be silent about the deaths of black fathers, uncles, and sons marched. We came together at the national seat of power and raised our voices, testifying to the necessity for activist, black public-sphere rededication on the part of and in the name of the *black majority*.

When we were called to a "Million Man March," the activist intellectual's choice was obvious, beyond debate, beyond cowardly public and published rationalizations that would make us *liked*. We who showed up were scarcely marching under the banners of Shorty or Griggs. We weren't looking for white men's elevators or meager coins in the nation's capital. That was not the goal of our fellowship. We came to stand under what we hoped were the approving eyes of our ancestors gone, black fathers, uncles, sons, mothers, sisters, aunts, and cousins who smiled down, mouthing perhaps those lyrics taught to us by my music teacher, Mrs. Carver, at Virginia Avenue Elementary School. We hoped black fathers of courage like my Uncle Vance might have found again their laughter on that day, at the march, spiritually present with us, reminding us that, indeed, stony has been "the road we trod." Rocks, aplenty.

On October 16, 1995, approximately one million black men (the numbers will always be in dispute) came together on the Mall in Washington, D.C. They were of varying hues, professions, classes, backgrounds, educational levels, hair types, dialects, ideologies, religions, geographies, affective styles, and emotional temperaments. The day was crystal clear: a gift from God. Fall sunshine warmed the earth where children slept peacefully at the feet of fathers, uncles, brothers—black men who had brought them to witness a striking exercise in American counterpoise. During the two weeks leading up to the march, pundits had relentlessly declared the event would be a balkanizing disaster for America. Black "public intellectuals" assured their white constituents and young black disciples that it was mandatory for any truly liberated, informed, and humane black man to separate the redemptive *message* of Minister Louis Farrakhan from the *messenger*. This, of course, made as much sense as saying: "Although President Bill Clinton implicitly endorsed an agenda that was Republican and insulted Lani Guinier, Sister Souljah, and Jocelyn Elders in public and endorsed welfare reform that wreaks havoc on black communities, let us separate the president himself from his message." It was difficult to tell if intellectuals who argued for a mind-body split of the message from the messenger were serious or simply offering solace to white audiences for pay. Did they really believe they could have a foot in both worlds? Did they believe they could stand tall for black redemption and simultaneously distance themselves from the only *mass* message being seriously listened to by black people in the United States? The black *mass* message was indeed issuing from the body of Farrakhan. "Body," in this instance, signifies both individual and institutional forms. For it is Farrakhan, the charismatic leader himself, who has rejuvenated and turned into a continuing force the body of the Nation of Islam following Elijah Muhammad's death in the 1970s. And it is the embodied black messenger himself who was the unambiguous presence par excellence on October 16, 1995.

Everyone on the Mall whom I encountered or moved among had eager expectations about the climactic moment at which Farrakhan would appear to articulate the notions of atonement, black manhood, responsibility, and community redemption that were goals of the Million Man March. To be sure, the march was a spiritual occasion. Like gatherings of the Promise Keepers (those Christian athletic men who assemble in huge stadiums across America to profess their faith), the October 16th assembly of black men was spiritually and, in a broad sense, religiously motivated. Still, it was the ministerial zest of Farrakhan, and no one else, that determined the spiritual flavor of the event.

So, what did pundits mean when they talked of separating the message from the messenger? Were they being playfully post-structuralist, suggesting perhaps the death of the orator: "What matter who speaks?"

What the separators hoped, I think, was to avoid a committed and forthright analysis of dangerous terrains—urban inner-city war zones and a desperately depressed black psyche in an era of American racial oppression. They hoped to serve as black filters for Farrakhanic "hate." One might argue that Farrakhan's articulations are more akin to what the black writer Ellis Cose calls "rage" than to "hate." But that is a point to be addressed later. For the moment, we might simply acknowledge the minister's downside. He has crafted a remarkable persona as a hatemonger. He has cunningly deployed a dark voice that targets *Jews* as the cause for the daily misery of the masses of black people in the United States. "Hold on!" we want to shout on encountering this persona. "What do you mean by *Jews*, Minister Farrakhan? Don't you know the word *Jew* has instigated some of the world's bleakest horrors?" But such an inquiry to Farrakhan would be akin to asking Newt Gingrich what he meant by *balanced budget*.

Balanced budget for Gingrich, like *Jews* for Farrakhan, represents an example of what the black critic Stephen Henderson refers to as a *mascon* word—a word that, like a sponge, absorbs the animus, bare intuition, disappointments, stereotypes, and rank feelings of superiority of a race. Mascon utterances don't allow for separation of the message from the messenger, the utterer from the utterance. Surely Newt's Contract With America cannot be separated from a radical Republican's body called Gingrich. Nor can it be separated from a mean-spirited, racialistic national agenda to make the white American body rich and richer while eliminating completely the nation's poor, elderly, and, in particular and most expressly, minorities. Likewise, it is impossible to separate Farrakhan's recourse to mascon scapegoating from a black *mass* constituency.

Yet who among us is in a position morally to forgive, filter, or separate a message of national oppression from the physical body of Newt Gingrich or William Jefferson Clinton? Who is in a position to condemn—with feigned innocence and incomprehension—Louis Farrakhan for expressing an entirely justifiable rage of a mass of black people targeted by the American fundamentalist and conservative Right for a white budget-balancing sacrifice? And who is so ethically precise that she or he can say: "Hey, black man, you better wear a sign down to that Washington march saying you separate the *message* from the *messenger*"?

Where is the sign around our own necks pronouncing on the

ignominy of a United States Congress, Supreme Court, and White House posturing before the full trough of "set asides" for big business in America and transnational capitalism in whiteface? Where are the luminescent signs strapped to our backs announcing precisely how we separate our president's and Congress's messages as "budget balancers" from their physical responsibility for the suffering of hundreds of thousands of federal employees and other unfortunate Americans struggling to hang on to homes, food, and life itself?

A flashback: Who remembers when the American nation writ large (whites in general)—but signed in lowercase by particularly Jewish "leaders"—called on all black people, and especially black intellectuals, to condemn, apologize, and sit abjectly in ashes at the crossroads because Khallid Abdul Muhammed made an inflammatory anti-Semitic speech at a college in New Jersey? Were the black people who then complied with such idiotic notions the same ones who called for the mind-body split with respect to Farrakhan and the Million Man March? Why do we as a black group have to apologize for individual decisions and follies?

On October 16, 1995, signs, buttons, shirts, hats, banners, posters, books, arm bands, personnel, and flags red-black-and-green, starred-and-crescented said: In organization and iconography this Million Man March is a Nation of Islam triumph in a symbolic war. This march is as complicated, multi-faceted, commonsensical, and surprising as the ability of Minister Louis Farrakhan to call it. Perhaps, then, the Minister *is* the capable *mass-concentrated* site of African American meaning in a time of war: a *War on Decency*.

Statistics of this War on Decency are by now well rehearsed, and everyone in America, as we shall shortly consider, has an opinion about who is to blame for America's general malaise. One in three black men in the United States is in prison, on parole, or under the supervision of the criminal justice system. More than half of black American children live in poverty. Black American income is only 60 percent that of white America. Black life expectancy is more than a decade shorter than white America's. Black youth unemployment is at 40 percent. Job opportunities and access to even minimal public services to sustain life are comparatively rare for most black Americans. Homicide and AIDS are killing young black men at staggering rates. Drugs are being pumped into black communities by rich profiteers like winter snow falling from laden skies.

Is the country at large outraged by the burdens and casualties of this War on Decency against black America? Is any constituency concerned, specifically, about the plight of black American men—young and old—and their unenviable condition in the United States? A sampling of the concerns of American cohorts other than black men gives some idea of what is on America's mind with respect to politics, persons, and events.

First, white men. What are they concerned about? Many of them are busy laying special claim to *anger* because, in their paranoid imaginations, blacks and women have it "so very good." A Million Man March would make no sense whatsoever to such men. Then there are white women. We saw, I believe, far too many of them televised at ritzy spas and glitzy espresso bars condemning the verdict and the defendant himself in the O. J. Simpson trial. Why? Because they felt Simpson had used his financial resources to beat a murder charge. Money was, suddenly, a bad thing of insidious influence. Did they see the Mall filled with the terror of a "million" O. J.'s?

Black women claimed prerogative to condemn the Million Man March, Louis Farrakhan, and the Nation of Islam because the Minister focused particular attention on the responsibilities, atonement, and sins of the fathers peculiar to that archetype some black women love to hate: *The Black Man.* "Women were excluded," commented some of the foremost intellectual black women in the United States. Was this naiveté, or did these women really *not* have a clue about the loci of the march in the mass approbation accorded gender discrimination in the Nation of Islam?

Then there were those black "public" spokespersons noted already who rushed to judgment in the name of principles of decency, coalition, cooperation, liberalism, and humaneness that have almost nothing to do with what one hopes is their *actual* sharp perception of America's War on Decency. Surely such black public intellectual spokespersons know that a war is in progress? These black intellectual men are, one has to assume, certainly aware of the statistics of war? Why, then, would they be reluctant to see the Million Man March as an act of resistance inseparable from Louis Farrakhan and the Nation of Islam? Were they afraid of some amorphous, threatening council of elders called the *Jews*? Scarcely. The motive of those famous black male public intellectuals who lamented the inseparability of the message and the messenger is clear. Their subject position *as* famous spokespersons—black guys who are *liked*—is bought and paid for by white men and women who wish to have their white egos and assumptions massaged by black boys and preaching entrepreneurs.

"Everybody," then, was against a joined-at-the-hip, message-and-messenger Million Man March. Everybody, that is, except a million black men who came to the Mall. Men who waited with quiet joy, easy dignity, and sober anticipation—standing at parade rest in October sunshine for twelve long hours—for the Messenger to appear and deliver his embodied blessing, challenge, and call to local social and political action.

Black men rode midnight trains and fourteen-hour chartered buses, drove Lexuses and Hondas and Mercedes and Tauruses and "hoopties" to the nation's capital to participate in an inseparable

ceremony in which the opinion of the most powerful black independent mass-oriented organization in America was repre-
sented by the messenger who called the march into existence. The
hundreds of thousands of black men who came were described
by the *Washington Post*—over and again—as "middle class." By
which the newspaper meant black men with serious jobs who
are not unaccounted for in official census rolls of this country.
Whether these black men were forthright or equivocal, practic-
ing Nation of Islam adherents or unabashedly independent, they
all sensed the inseparability of message and messenger. For it was
this inseparability that—in any rational or practical account of
the Million Man March—caused them to chant as the hour grew
near: "FARRAKHAN, FARRAKHAN, FARRAKHAN!" "Middle
class black men" calling for the Messenger. Did they call for
Farrakhan because they endorsed a gospel of hate, a philosophy
of scapegoating *Jews*? No. In part their chant was, quite simply,
the verbal representation of a distinctively American "Black Man
Thing." It was the sounded intensity of a peculiarly American
manifestation of rage and desire. It was about lost sons and dying too early.

Returning for a moment to Ellis Cose and his book *The Rage
of a Privileged Class*, we find the following story of a "middle class"
middle-aged law-firm partner's encounter with the rituals of
black success in America:

> One source of immense resentment was [his] encounter of a few
> days previous, when he had arrived at the office an hour or so
> earlier than usual and entered the elevator along with a young
> white man. They got off at the same floor. No secretaries or
> receptionists were yet in place. As my friend [black partner] fished
> in a pocket for his key card while turning toward the locked outer
> office doors, his elevator mate blocked his way and asked, "May I

help you?" My friend shook his head and attempted to circle around his would-be [white] helper, but the young man stepped in front of him and demanded in a loud and decidedly colder tone, "May I help you?" At this, the older man fixed him with a stare, spat out his name, and identified himself as a partner, whereupon his inquisitor stepped aside. My friend's initial impulse was to put the incident behind him, to write it off as merely another annoyance in an ordinary day. Yet he had found himself growing angrier and angrier at the young associate's temerity. . . . "Because of his color, he felt he had the right to check me out."[8]

A later formulation by Cose succinctly captures the implicit structures of his friend's experience: "Whatever difficulties Americans may have thinking of blacks as potential CEOs, no particular imagination is required [for whites] to visualize crime with an African-American face" (93). The young white man's assumption of criminal trespass on the part of his better dressed, older, and extremely well-heeled black companion is symbolic of white America's leap to the criminal accusation and treatment that enrages black men in America in virtually all rounds of their daily lives—regardless of class, temperament, or bank accounts. The moment of rage closest to the Million Man March was white America's lynch-mob response to the verdict in the O. J. Simpson murder trial.

Candle-burning mobs of middle-class whites assembled on street corners and at television studios to call for "real" justice. By which they meant—at least—the incarceration of a wealthy black megastar who had married one of their own and moved into their neighborhood. At worst, they meant: *String up the black bastard!* The divide between whites and blacks with respect to the O. J. verdict was as decisive an indicator as any black man could find that white folks are now full of temerity and as ready as the blast of a .38 to prevent criminal trespass by blacks to conditions of decent living in the United States. A white War on Decency is in full, vigilante effect.

There was, then, a raging Black Man Thing motivating chants of *Farrakhan!* Many who assembled on the Mall knew the Minister would articulate—publicly and at a globally televised symbolic site—their own discontent. Such public articulation they felt was cathartic and necessary, indeed, indispensable—because most black men don't have country clubs or country-club estates in gated communities, or unlicensed authority and secretiveness in which to batter their wives and desert their children in the name of "job stress" like so very many white men do. Because most black men don't have the privilege or luxury of awaking to just another day in which they can ignore the *New York Times* and *Wall Street Journal* and still know, like so many white men, that nobody is coming to get *them* in the morning. "Spindling boys," like the white elevator clerk at the law firm, look in the mirror any time of day, see white skin, and are reassured of their superiority—their regal supremacy.

More than a logic of rage and discontent, however, was involved in the chanting summons for the Messenger to appear. In a year when Allen and Albert Hughes's film *Dead Presidents* toured nationally, it would have been shocking if black public spokespersons did not realize that Farrakhan transformed—through pure genius and inspiration—the Mall into a front line of symbolic political warfare. Farrakhan clearly understood that such warfare needs massive troops of black American men, the same race of men who have served eternally as cannon fodder for American wars: Indian Wars, Spanish American, World Wars I and II, Korea, Vietnam. The Minister was proleptic. He knew the future story (as opposed to the *Toy Story*) of current American symbolic warfare against people of color: "In Mount Pleasant [a neighborhood of the nation's capital], a group of about fifty Latinos gathered yesterday morning at a soccer field on 16th Street NW and unfurled a banner that said, 'Latino Solidarity with the Million Man March'.... 'We've never had anything in common with Louis Farrakhan, but we're in a war and we need allies,' said Pedro Aviles, executive director of the Latino Civil Rights Task Force, which organized the contingent" (*Washington Post*, October 17, 1995, A20).

Farrakhan "reappropriated" the Mall as the ideological turf of American decency that black American men must defend—in the absence of historical and present-day "decency" on the part of white American men.

Farrakhan began his overly long oration by pointing mystically to symbolic monuments named *Jefferson, Washington, Lincoln*. He went on to weave a tapestry of numerical speech acts, focusing his troops' attention on the monumentality of horror that is the American Founding Fathers' and the American presidency's white supremacy. Earlier in the day, Reverend Jesse Jackson had tried to rouse the troops by eliding October 16th with the Birmingham, Alabama, civil rights events of another era. He claimed the march's actual "messengers" were Newt Gingrich and Bob Dole. A young black man standing near me said: "Jesse ought to go platinum with his old-school stuff. We got a pastor just like Jesse at our church. One of those Old Boys. We have to raise our hands two hours into his sermon and say: 'Reverend Johnson, you do know the game is on, don't you?'"

Even before Reverend Jackson's speech, President William Jefferson Clinton had stood before a mostly white audience in Texas and invoked Presidents Abraham Lincoln and Lyndon

Johnson to talk about previous moments of American racial "divide." He pontificated about how the American presidency had worked always toward national "union." But Clinton did not offer a single American presidential dollar, strategy, or promise that might constitute a significant intervention in today's American War on Decency. Now, as the young brother said, Jesse may be vintage platinum. But Clinton was strictly, with his nostalgia for Lincoln and Johnson, a golden oldies man.

Farrakhan's oration was a brilliant stroke of numerology, a masterpiece of symbolic politics. He spoke in an era of sound-bite, antiblack warfare. An era that has witnessed a remarkable and horrifying angry white voter turnout. A turnout manipulated to hatred by a politics of blame that cynically produces images of Willie Horton, white hands crumpling job rejection letters produced by affirmative action, and a wildly out of control American "crime" in blackface. In such an era how can a useful black agenda ignore, or reject, countersymbolic political warfare? No one has been more effective at such counterwarfare than Louis Farrakhan.

The Million Man March was not Farrakhan's *only,* but it was certainly his most *effective* symbolic campaign. Two days after the march, he announced that the Nation of Islam—for the first time in that organization's history—would be actively involved in American electoral politics. If Ross Perot, Ralph Reed, and Pat Buchanan, then why not Louis Farrakhan?

However, the politics of the Million Man March were not exclusive. Everybody—Marxists, Leninists, advocates for black economic development, defenders of Mumia Abu-Jamal, voter registration adherents, Civil Rights Movement Christians—everybody had a political and cultural forum on October 16, 1995. Thanks to the Call to the Mall, some black men had their first acquaintance with political agendas, strategies, and events relevant to black America unknown before all-night bus trips from Georgia hamlets, Detroit suburbs, American college and university campuses, and Chicago ghettos. The men and women who delivered formal addresses from the stage in front of the Capitol outlined expansive and varied ranges of political, social, and spiritual programs. Hundreds of thousands of black men (and some women) stood, listened, and paid attention.

What has transpired on local levels since the Washington march? Reverend Jesse Jackson brought to his television show black men who spoke passionately about local urban organizations either founded or given additional financial and personnel resources by the Million Man march. In Philadelphia, young black men have organized a black economic development agency.

Oh, yes, there have been some concrete, positive, local results.

By the close of his address, Louis Farrakhan had each member of his symbolically armed regiments ready to take an oath: "I, Houston Baker . . ." Yes, I was an advocate for and participant in the march. There was for me no logical possibility of separating, in a time of war, the message from the messenger. Louis Farrakhan, chief spokesperson for the most expansive independent organization of black Americans in these United States, has managed to stay alive and active. That is a miracle of no small proportions.

I went to the Million Man March with the support of my family. My mother and mother-in-law sat enthralled all day on October 16th by C-SPAN's coverage of the event. My brothers called the night before to convey a single message: *Represent.* My son said: "Dad, you know if I were anywhere near we'd be going together." All of this I interpreted to mean: There is a war going on in these United States. The message and the messenger of the Million Man March stand in a relationship best captured by the

Reverend Joseph Lowery when he said on the Sunday before the march: "If my house is on fire, I don't care who brings the water." As fate and an American politics of blame would have it, God gave Minister Farrakhan the "rainbow sign." There is precious little water for the burning house of most of black America. Unless we take symbolically armed, forthright, thoughtful local action now in our own black interests and self-defense, the fire next time of global capitalism will consume us utterly.

As his last words echoed over the Mall, I turned from Farrakhan and the group of extraordinary black American men with whom I had shared field duty for a day. I headed for home. I thought about what I had witnessed: Amazing scenes of young black children sleeping on the warm October ground at the feet of men who had brought them to the Mall. Teenagers in hoodies and skull-caps and baggy jeans who tipped reverently by these sleeping youngsters, as though the ground on which they rested were hallowed. Single files of black men, hands on the shoulders of the person in front, zigzagging through crowds of a hundred thousand black men who politely and quietly parted for them. I heard a young man behind me say: "Excuse me, sir, do you mind if I smoke?" The "sir" was me. His was an uncommonly polite gesture since we were standing in the open air. On October 16, 1995, I watched black men embrace, weep, listen, stand tall, feel simply and confidently relaxed in each other's presence. We looked at ourselves, our children, all our brothers on that day. We knew the American war in which we were engaged, and for that "moment" were not afraid. We blessed our fathers. Prayed to be strong in times of need for all our black children under assault by those who normally own the Mall and use its offices to *clear* America of "strangers" such as us.

End Thought

"Think of the Days of the Past,

Learn from the Past"

Within weeks after the march on Washington, Minister Farrakhan announced that the Nation of Islam would seriously enter the lists of American electoral politics. However, the most notable post-Washington Farrakhan news surrounded the leader's excursion into territories and domains of strongmen and dictatorial heads of states such as Saddam Hussein and Muammar al-Qaddafi. American outcry and condemnation greeted this flagrant trespass of the protocols of black diplomatic likability. Farrakhan's strange house calls upon dictators instantly rendered him the evil twin of the likable Reverend Jesse Jackson, who seems chronically addicted to white photo opportunities for moral punditry, hostage release, and prayer with foreign villains in the name of the fathers of Christian democracy.

Clearly it is disconcerting to envision dollars willingly shelled out by black fathers and sons on the Mall financing manic sojourns of Mr. Farrakhan into repressive lands. And who, after all, has actually seen a published audit of the Million Man March's account ledgers? Rumor has it the Minister suffered physical and psychological strain par excellence after his day on the Mall, becoming something of a Southwest recluse. Needless to say, those black fathers and sons who attempted to carry forth stated logics of the march in their own hometowns must have been nonplussed—both by the strange diplomacy and mysterious withdrawal of Farrakhan from American public life.

In Philadelphia, fathers and sons organized and marched in

support of the last black-owned supermarket, their battle flag announcing that they did so in the "Spirit of the Million Man March." In North Carolina, black men and their sons canvassed communities, urging parents to buy health insurance rather than Christmas presents for their children. And in his film *Get on the Bus*, Spike Lee endeavored to explore the manifold logics of the march as an American event. Imitators of Farrakhan and the Nation of Islam madly scrambled to duplicate the Minister's Call to the Mall, instituting "million body" marches in the name of myriad organizations, constituencies, and causes—including black youth. In the year 2000, it is "Moms." Such efforts have met with but indifferent success—though Philadelphia's "Million Woman March" drew kudos from some quarters. What seems preeminently to remain of that glorious October day in 1995 is memory. There remains as well an occasion for critique inspired by such memory.

Looking back on the march from the vantage of our turn-of-the-millennium moment, the spectacle seems both an ironic watershed and a sad memorial to the classic dramaturgy of mass black protest and reform so integral to any definition of twenti-eth-century radical politics in the United States. The less-than-glorious aftermath of the Farrakhan march suggests, perhaps, that the Minister's day in the sun may well have been the last American instance of a mass and spirited body-on-the-line politics by a black majority presence in the United States. Jesse Jackson proclaimed on the Mall that the Million Man March was produced—indeed made inevitable—by a new, racialized, uncompromising white American conservatism (remember the congressional "Republican Revolution" of 1995?).

Today, Reverend Jackson's proclamation seems prophecy. For, just as surely as the assembly of black fathers and sons on the Mall appeared to be almost a *natural* continuation of public-sphere and civil rights strategies and impulses of American radical politics of the 1960s, so today, in the United States, such an assembly seems utterly inconceivable. The "visible white hand" of conservatism invoked by Jesse Jackson has become a full-bodied and unforgiving corporatist arbiter in politics, finance, media, jurisprudence, law enforcement, entertainment, housing, and college and university enrollment and curriculum in America.

What seemingly has disappeared from every real (and almost every imaginable) channel is precisely any word, sign, presence, or deed of the majority of black Americans. Absent as well are virtually any imaginative conceptualizations or strategies (of *any* kind) for seriously enhancing the public-sphere empowerment of the black majority. William Julius Wilson's extraordinary ethnography of the black poor of Chicago's South Side, *When Work Disappears*, offers a bleak cartography of depressed economic, social, and emotional states of the black majority in America. Black majority terrain is marked by open-air drug marts, black-on-black homicides, homelessness, AIDS, mental illness without hope of treatment, and crumbling lives of hideous desperation. North Philadelphia, like East Durham and South Central Los Angeles, are genuinely *no* places to be *somebody*. Zones of black majority confinement and abjection in the United States are today the silenced "norm."

Where is the critical memory, we might inquire, needed to resurrect hope or promise of even minimal intervention in the relentless American mapping of black confinement, deprivation, and social death?

My answer, perhaps, is predictable. Having commenced with the wisdom and boldness of Richard Wright's injunction and example to black men and women of articulateness and literacy to rage against the dying of the light, I can do no more than conclude with Wright. Wright made his way from the Mississippi

Delta to podiums of international address. Along the way, he never forgot his was an inescapable mission. He *always* remembered that black public mobility and articulateness were rare (and endangering) attainments in the United States. Wright thus refused to squander social and political opportunities for intervention. He seemed almost genetically programmed, one might say, against sycophantic bids merely to be liked. . . . and he paid in full. An autodidact of a brilliant cast, he sought always to articulate comprehensive memorial models for the black writer/ scholar's work, models that would be interventionist, instructive, realizable . . . productive in advancing a global black majority's quest for a good life.

Out of the evidence of his own life, and far from blessed with the multitude of options belonging to our turn-of-the-millennium's black *minority* (that is, the always and forever "new" black middle class), Wright refused to erase the lessons or ignore the deep psychological lesions of the preeminent locale of black culture formation in America—namely, the South. If, as James Baldwin suggested in an arch postmortem, Wright remained all of his days a mischievous "Mississippi pickaninny," surely Wright must have always been confidently self-conscious in this American masquerade, indeed, internationally "radical" in such a guise in a manner that remained forever beyond the comprehension and effective reach of Baldwin's own pen.

What are the entailments of the example of Richard Wright upon our present-day lives and memory? I think they are as simple and dangerous for black men and women of privilege in the United States as they have ever been. WE who are positioned in business, commerce, Congress, law, labor, finance, marketing, academics; we who live in comfortable spaces of the black dream within a dream that is U.S. black middle-class existence; we who send our sons into the streets or yards outside comfortable homes and never worry about drive-by-shootings or other horrors; we who have never seen the inside of a correctional facility; we whose paycheck is as certain as the rising and setting sun . . . we, WE are now the last best hope and potential resource for twenty-first-century renewal of possibilities for public-sphere empowerment and good life advantages for the black American majority.

Welfare, affirmative action, food-stamp philanthropy, black neighborhood renewal, health care, and antidrug drives will *not* be legacies to the black majority from the white politics, polity, and policy of the land where we all, at one time or another, hold our breaths, hoping white structures holding power over our lives will for another day, week, year continue to find us likable.

As demographics shift in the United States and blacks fade from their position as the "dominant" or most populous minority interest group, so the spotlight on the black majority's needs fades.

Only commitment to critical memory by those of us positioned to enlighten first ourselves and then others can intervene in the American clearance and confinement that are now the dominant motions of politics and finance with respect to the black majority in the United States.

Surely the notion of an articulate black elite as the most important resource for the enhancement of the status of the black majority is far from a new or original notion. After all, W. E. B. Du Bois's proposal for a "talented tenth" was merely a variation on a theme that has been omnipresent in black American culture for men and women of talent and advantage for generations. However, what is so significant at the present time about a commitment to critical memory by well-positioned blacks is the direct, in-our-face, assaultive regimen of U.S. law, politics, and finance that marks the turn of the millennium. It is finally a realization that black sons and fathers not only die too early in the United States, but also that a present-day United States is geared toward such deaths . . . it is this realization that must send us back to activist archives and our long repertoires of black survival, black progress songs, strategies, deeds, and events in order to guard what remains of and is possible for a black majority good life in the United States.

Racial profiling is not simply a matter of huge numbers of blacks being detained under dubious law-enforcement constraints of DWB (driving while black). No, O, No: racial profiling, as the millennium turns, means the optically and electronically surveilled, databased *placing* of all American blacks in the crosshairs of a new dynamics of identity. "New," but really . . . very, very old. We—especially we who are privileged with steady paychecks—are being told paradoxically that if we are to be liked *as blacks*, we must not only forget the majority of those in the United States who are, in fact, black, but also relinquish all thoughts of an American past where the reality for the entire majority of sons and fathers of blackness was slavery, convict lease labor, menial employment, second-class citizenship, social death, and immobilizing poverty.

I suggest that for the first time ever in U.S. history, we who are privileged have no excuse but fear, greed, comfortable indolence, or callous indifference for either forgetting or thinking soberly that being *liked* as a black man in America is in any way equated with his being safe, or guaranteeing the safety of his sons, who continue to go to American boot camps, jails, prisons . . . to die too early. What has changed and what gives us cause for optimism is our numbers and our sites of enunciation and possible intervention—not to mention the real fiscal and cultural capital now available to us.

Yes, as a black middle class, we are more numerous and better positioned and resourced than we have ever been in the United

States. Which, in one sense, heightens as dramatically as ever the vast discrepancy between what we seem to have achieved of security and safety and the fact that we have never been more endangered. The present media networks' situations with respect to blacks is indicative of the level of what might be called our deep eradication from the circuits of American day-to-day consciousness. There is, literally, almost *nobody* black to be seen on major television network programming. And the programming of almost all channels of American life contains at least an implicit desire to mirror television networks' contented, calculated, corporatist *disappearing act* vis-à-vis blacks.

Deuteronomy enjoins us to "think of the days of the past, learn from the past." If we who, like Richard Wright, are literate and have social opportunity to profit from archives of black writers, race men and race women who left examples of strategic, articulate, courageous interventions in America's "clearance" and derogation of the black majority—if we move now to "heed but the past" we may prevail. If we structure our commitments to accord critically and memorially with the best of our past, there is just a chance black fathers and sons may yet gather again in legions, genuinely about the business of redeeming ourselves and bringing the majority out of the dread darkness of confinement and into a good life in the light of a twenty-first-century American day.

Notes

1. Richard Wright, *Black Boy (American Hunger): A Record of Childhood and Youth* (New York: Perennial Classics, 1998), 270. All citations refer to this edition and are hereafter marked by page numbers in parentheses.

2. Jerry Gafio Watts, *Heroism and the Black Intellectual: Ralph Ellison, Politics, and Afro-American Intellectual Life* (Chapel Hill: University of North Carolina Press, 1994), 86. All citations hereafter are marked by page numbers in parentheses.

3. Daryl C. Dance, "You Can't Go Home Again: James Baldwin and the South," *CLA Journal* 18 (1974): 81–90.

4. Ida B. Wells-Barnett, *Crusade for Justice: The Autobiography of Ida B. Wells*, ed. Alfreda M. Duster (Chicago: University of Chicago Press, 1970), 42.

5. Christopher John Farley, "Seriously Funny," *Time* (Sept. 13, 1999), 66–70.

6. Ralph Ellison, *Invisible Man* (New York: Vintage International, 1990), 34. All citations refer to this edition and are hereafter marked by page numbers in parentheses.

7. Richard Wright, *12 Million Black Voices* (New York: Thunder's Mouth Press, 1988), 117. All citations refer to this edition and are hereafter marked by page numbers in parentheses.

8. Ellis Cose, *The Rage of a Privileged Class* (New York: Harper Perennial, 1995), 48–49. All citations hereafter are marked by page numbers in parentheses.